NEVADANS

NEVADANS

by ROLLAN MELTON

Foreword by Robert Laxalt

Portraits by Christine Stetter

UNIVERSITY OF NEVADA PRESS

RENO *&* LAS VEGAS

*Publication of this book was made possible
by a grant from Nancy and Robert Cashell.*

*The paper used in this book meets the requirements of American National Standard
for Information Sciences—Permanence of Paper for Printed Library Materials,
ANSI Z39.48–1984. Binding materials were chosen for strength and durability.*

Library of Congress Cataloging-in-Publication Data

Melton, Rollan, 1931–
Nevadans / by Rollan Melton; foreword by Robert Laxalt; drawings
by Christine Stetter.
p.   cm.
Newspaper columns previously published in the Reno gazette-journal
and the Reno evening gazette, 1978–1987.
Includes index.
ISBN 0-87417-143-1 (alk. paper)
ISBN 0-87417-142-3 (pbk.: alk. paper)
1. Nevada—Social life and customs.   2. Nevada—Biography.
I. Title.
F845.M45   1988   979.3'033'0922—dc 19   88-17755   CIP

University of Nevada Press, Reno, Nevada 89557 USA
Copyright © Rollan Melton 1988
All rights reserved
Book and cover design by Dave Comstock
Printed in the United States of America

9 8 7 6 5 4 3 2 1

To my wife Marilyn,
whose enormous talents include
lighting my way

Contents

Foreword _____

WHAT AUTHOR ROLLAN MELTON has managed to craft in this book is a mosaic of the personality, character and attitudes of the true Nevadan—whether by birth or by choice.

Glimpses of that Nevadan glint through each story and each profile in singularly revealing brush strokes. The secret, of course, is one that Rollan Melton is not aware of—that only a Nevadan by rearing and perception, and with sensitivity to the state's people and settings, could have written this book.

We see the great and the little, the famous and the unknown. Through their exploits and tragedies and in their all-revealing speech, they form an integral part of the mosaic.

We see important men such as silver-maned Pat McCarran, in his time the most powerful U.S. senator. The difference from the ordinary view is that we see him through the awed eyes of a teenage apprentice printer in a small Nevada town, Fallon. The youth is properly impressed, but with the clear vision of the young, he is surprised that McCarran is a short, stocky man, no taller than himself, not a ten-foot giant.

Side by side with the famous, we see an unsung mailman in the little Nevada hamlet of Austin, and we follow him through dust and blizzards and washed-out roads. The deeds of Reese Gandolfo delivering the U.S. mail will never be recorded in high history, but the author has given him his proper due here.

So also are etched the diverse personalities of Nevada history:

—Raymond I. "Pappy" Smith, the one-time carnival barker who came to Reno and took gambling out of the back rooms and into the national limelight, by transforming a hole-in-the-wall into Harolds Club.

—football coach Jake Lawlor, a relentless tyrant and a gentle father-confessor whose "fixed stare stabbed us like tracer bullets."

—Judge Ted Lunsford, the town of Elko's "Marryin' Sam," who in his lifetime married 50,000 couples.

—Dr. Fred Anderson, who began his education in a one-room schoolhouse and went on to become a Rhodes scholar and an eminent surgeon.

—Nancy Gomes and Mary Gojack, legislators and champions of women's rights until their deaths from cancer.

—towering Ben Dasher, one of the biggest targets at the Normandy invasion, and his incredible lifetime contributions to public causes.

—Willie Capucci, Fallon's collector of Nevada memorabilia, a veritable pack rat who suffers mingled emotions when his collection is auctioned off.

We take a walk with Jack Dempsey, the world heavyweight boxing champion who once lived and fought in Reno. We spend an unforgettable evening in the farming community of Wellington, boasting "a grocery store, a bar-restaurant and little else"—except for its plain-speaking people and their views of the world outside. We share a conversation between Lieutenant Governor Bob Cashell and his perceptive wife Nancy and Phyllis Diller. We are silent witnesses to the solitary after-hours writing of editorials by Paul Leonard, tireless editor of the *Nevada State Journal*.

And in a powerful, understated vignette, we see how the attack on Pearl Harbor in 1941 affected small-town America. The news traveled not by television but by word of mouth, house to house. Before the war ended, thirty-six Gold Stars hung in the living rooms of Fallon, a community of only two thousand souls.

It is said that every state and every region in the United States has its particular brand of humor. Nevada's wry, Twainesque humor is captured here by Rollan Melton. From an era gone by, we read the nicknames of White Pine County—Antler Joe, Seldom Seen Slim, and Tiger Flowers.

The sounds and smells and seasons of Nevada have their place, too, from blazing summer to the falling leaves of autumn, unexpectedly surprising the reader with their poetry. "Low-slung hills venture into dusk, taking on hues of pink and lavender and olive green."

Author Rollan Melton's final story is called "Loving Each Newspaper Day." It is the born newspaperman speaking now, tracing his career from fifteen-year-old apprentice printer (and janitor) to journalism student, army correspondent, cub reporter, sports reporter, editor, publisher of Reno newspapers, member of the board of directors of the massive Gannett media chain (and its senior vice-president) back to where he wanted to be all along—at his typewriter.

What he forgot to say was that through his writings, he has become the man who captured the old heart of Nevada before it is gone forever.

ROBERT LAXALT

Preface _____

THE GENESIS OF THIS BOOK is my boyhood in Nevada. I landed in Fallon when I was fourteen, after moving with my people from state to state. I had been in eighteen schools by the time I staggered through the eighth grade. It wasn't long after arrival in Nevada that I knew my drifting was ended, so this became my first real home.

For all the following years, from 1945 until now, I have studied Nevada and its wonderful people, admired the new Nevadans and the old, seeing them as a distinct breed, knowing that they are here by choice. I am blessed because I have had the incredible good fortune to tell their stories.

In my fledgling newspaper years in Fallon, in Sparks, at the University of Nevada and with Reno dailies, I wrote every day, specializing in people profiles. I decided early that I wanted to be a columnist and I did write a column for the *Sagebrush* on the Reno campus. Later, as a young *Reno Evening Gazette* sports editor, I wrote a thrice-weekly column.

But then, my bosses dragged me from my writing machine and had me anchored to an administrative desk. There I stayed for fourteen years, loving the exciting challenge of leadership. But all the time, I yearned to go back to the people and the telling of their stories.

Ten years ago, I made the move back to writing. At first, I was surprised that my words wouldn't flow as once they had. Whatever skills I possessed had been dulled by those mountains of memos, reports and securities-analyst speeches I had been doing for so long. As the saying goes: Use it or lose it. Finally, I was able to shake the carbon out of my writing system, and survive.

Nearly two thousand Rollan Melton columns have since emerged from my aged Underwood. The Nevadans who have shared their words, wit and wisdom have made this the happiest period of my happy newspaper life.

I never thought I was constructing a book while doing my daily duty. The published column vignettes have mounted steadily and so has the accumulated stack of ideas yet to research and write. But in 1987, my wife Marilyn suggested the time had arrived to think of a book of columns.

Another piece of good fortune—the University of Nevada Press agreed to publish the book.

The most difficult task has been to winnow my *Reno Gazette-Journal* columns to a manageable number. We are talking about an aggregate of a million and a half written words, or fifteen good-sized books. The process of elimination tore me up as stories of great Nevadans were put aside, out of necessity. Hard as I tried, I couldn't convince anyone to make these decisions for me. I am responsible for the final selections.

I tried to make the eighty-eight columns that appear here representative of my published work over the past decade.

Thanks very much for reading.

Acknowledgments ————————————

FOR YEARS I HAVE LISTENED with little sympathy as author friends have told of their loathing to write the "acknowledgments" section at the forepart of their books.

Now I understand their anxiety. It is my turn to squirm.

This is the moment of truth, time to set down the names of all who helped give birth to this printed baby. In my case, a list of everyone who ever taught me, lifted me, offered very necessary criticism, helped me out of jams, been my friend—goodness, the list of my helpers would be as long as this book!

But let me name a few.

A writing style is forged in one's early years. Mine was first supported by my high school benefactor-teacher, Anne Gibbs Berlin, and by my wondrous weekly *Fallon Standard* role models, Claude H. Smith and Kenneth A. Ingram; friends Barbara and Carl Shelly not only let me make boy-reporter mistakes at the *Sparks Tribune,* but paid me for them; Keiste Janulis and Alfred L. Higginbotham gave me the finest university journalism education a young Nevada man could hope for; and my Nevada-Reno English professor, Robert Gorrell, has my lasting gratitude for giving me vital lessons while I was young.

My debt to Reno newspaper editorial executive colleagues cannot be adequately repaid. The unsung heroes include Joseph R. Jackson, John Sanford, Charles G. Murray, Charles H. Stout, Robert N. Nitsche, Warren L. Lerude, Robert B. Whittington, Sue Clark Jackson, Paul A. Leonard and Ty Cobb.

During my *Reno Gazette-Journal* columnist period, from October 8, 1978, to the present, I have been supported enthusiastically by executive editors Robert Ritter, Barbara Henry and Everett Landers, each steadfast with patience and help; superior editing, giving me a sound court of last resort, came from William O'Driscoll, William Cieslewicz, Jeannie Rasmussen, Joe DeChick, Tonia Cunning and Guy Richardson.

I often lean heavily on our newspaper librarians and would flounder without Nancy Spina, Carole Keith and William Henricks.

My secretary, Mickey Wessel, is a super talent and an indispensable supporter and ally, saving me from countless writing embarrassments.

I am fortunate to have the counsel of writing-publishing expert Myrick "Mike" Land and of incomparable author Robert Laxalt.

My Reno newspaper production friends have been unstinting in their help these many years, especially Lee Overpeck, Lee Schennum, Helen Sewell, Ralph Rhodes and Larry Urrutia.

The University of Nevada Press, heavy on individual talent, provided me with superior allies in Kathryn Gude, Nicholas Cady, director John "Rick" Stetter, and Cameron Sutherland.

A great executive leader, Allen H. Neuharth, chairman of the global Gannett Company, blessed my 1978 decision to leave corporate ranks and return to writing, and he has supported me in countless ways.

To Nancy and Robert Cashell, extraordinary Nevadans and friends, my lasting thanks for all good deeds.

This book has been a family endeavor. My wife Marilyn ran interference with my publisher, and our daughter Emelie was a star at the word processor in the early editing process.

My keenest thanks to the thousands of Nevada reader-friends who have supported me with their ideas, praise and criticism. This is their book and I thank them for everything.

HOME MEANS NEVADA

Nevada

A TOAST, on the eve of her 115th birthday, to our beloved Nevada:

Here's to the Nevada so little known to those who've not lived within her boundaries, or to those unlucky souls who are yet to ride and hike her distant parts. Let us toast her burbling creeks and gorgeous wildflowers, her seemingly endless space, made so joyous by those quiet, lovely valleys, and let us pay respects to her rising summits, a thorough test for even the bravest of radiators.

Queen desert state of the Far West, thirty-sixth admitted to the Union, and appearing at first glimpse to be the lunar landscape. But wait! There is the palette of colors spilled on barren form. Great shadows pounce out of nowhere to sweep across our land, a sur-realistic landscape painted on living canvas, with her secrets waiting to be whispered to the fortunate viewer.

Low-slung hills venture into dusk, taking on hues of pink and lav-ender and olive green. And our larger mountains, not the fir-covered grand dames of the Sierra, but those to the north, south and east—such rugged beauty, and always changing. Now they are mouse-brown, later blotched by grays and blacks. Are they now turned to steely gray? Yes, but then they glow red-pink-gold.

Nevada: it has been speculated unkindly that God created her last among the fifty states, using only the leftovers. But the bumper sticker denounces that cruel rumor: "God don't make junk." Rather, what He gave us are the geographic textures, sounds and smells that add up to pleasures to be remembered.

Here's to her sounds: the crow of the cock pheasant at dawn's early light; the warning *brrrrrt* of the coiled rattler; the *charrrrrugggh* of bullfrogs in the tules on a summer night; that whir of chukar sur-prised at a watering hole. Or the night or daytime toot of the freight train.

Here's to the smell of her freshly cut alfalfa and the odor of sage-brush after the rainstorm. Take a whiff of wild lupine and columbine

3

and forget-me-nots and shooting stars, Indian paintbrush and delphinium, and you won't be displeased. But getting downwind from drainage points and alkali flats might be something else.

Let's hear it for sitting around a campfire at Bean Flat, listening to coyotes howl and drinking java from an old tin can. Let's hear cheers for the beauty of the Austin Summit.

Here's to the twinkling stars, still so clearly visible away from the metropolitan smog patches at either end of the state. Here's to the little streams that with a bit more encouragement will become creeks. Let's hear it for Nevada's watercress at the spring's mouth, for mountain meadows accessible to those willing and able to explore afoot and for those lovely wild geraniums in Big Smoky Valley.

Nevada: dust devils playing footsie in the desert playground; and east of Fallon gigantic Sand Mountain, which is really not so overwhelming unless you're inspired by zillions of grains of sand; land of man's planted fields and sweet sunsets and memorable rainbows and every few weeks a gorgeous moon. The viewing of antelope grazing in hayfields is commonplace in Nevada.

Let's hear it for the saffron yellow of autumn-blooming rabbit brush; for our pungent sage; the music of the desert wind; our four-season luxury. Is there anything finer than 95-degree maximums, with but hints of humidity? Let's hear it for huge batches of sunshine, generous doses of unbeatable Nevada autumns, with accompanying spectacular color shows. Let us toast the generous snowpacks—may they forever bless us. Together we thank the One Who is responsible for these very big spaces in which to work and play.

Finally, let us toast Nevadans: here's to their general axiom, "Waste not, want not." To their perseverance, passed on by the grace of genes and training. To their wisdom: "Be careful what you wish for—you may get it."

Here's to Nevadans' individualism: "In our state there's enough room to make a damn fool out of yourself and nobody will bother stopping you."

Nevada: the state that grows its own rodeo stock and its own cowboys and the place where the drugstore dude is laughed at to his face.

A birthday toast to Nevada and her people: to the rugged beauty of a great state and to its great residents—the old-timers, the newcomers and those in between. May all of us come to love our state even more, for she will prosper if we treat her right.

4

Summer ————————————————

GLORIOUS NEVADA SUMMER, it revisits us at last, blessed, delicious and as spectacular as always. A summer in Nevada—that's nature replaying one of her nicest miracles. We are the beneficiaries, and oh how lucky we are!

The evidence is every place now. Given the generous wetness of our winter and spring, we enjoy the green, green grass at home and through the parks, the meadows and the ranges. Pretty blossoms, burgeoning shrubs and the trees have burst from hibernation.

Could any summer be finer than those enjoyed around these parts? Well, hardly. We have this to savor until autumn gently nips us. And we're ready. Ready and eager for the sun god to sprinkle us with magic. Ready to yield to the scent of summer, to lap up the spirited yells of the vacationing children, prepared for what is always one of Nevada's most pleasant seasonal treats. Time for some more midyear weather glory. Tolerable high-noon heat, most pleasant dawns and quick-cooling dusks. And the humidity? Again, thankfully, it is slim or none.

See the summer signals. The swimming places of northern Nevada, jammed to the gills with young human tadpoles. School's out and it's so swell and summer's in and it's so grand. Here, we view armadas of invading tourist buses—there, columns of marchers, hikers, strollers. Over there, a fresh wave of joggers, come to tune out the rust and drink in the sunshine. Boats of all descriptions, folks of all sizes and fishermen with varying luck along the Truckee and at Pyramid and Tahoe. Invaders from bordering states, marching in for another glimmering season of fun indoors and out.

Amid the arriving tourist army are sprinkled our own Nevadans. Proud of their state and with patented bragging rights on this very special summer season. Smiling, nodding knowingly every time an out-of-stater says, "I hope you know how lucky you are living here." A comment heard over and over. We know! What other area serves up such consistently smiling sky? Cooling summer breezes? No other place, U.S.A., that's where.

The Nevada summer sounds are all around now in our playland. The hum of the inbound camper trucks and the roar of rejuvenated boat engines, coming alive after long months of sleeping. The straining cowboys, the scampering rodeo clowns and "Here he comes folks, Willie Western, riding out of Chute No. 4." Highways crowded by people lured here by the promise of sun, fun and motion. A ton of summer satisfaction, that's all they yearn for. And they'll get it. Again.

We must accept the summer bad with the good. A few million extra tourists, maneuvering for elbow and knee room, for instance. And in Nevada places where abatement is slack, there's a raft of blood-lusting mosquitoes. On our hottest days, the temperature might exceed 100 degrees and we'll grumble, but it's strictly momentary. Comes again the merciful dusk, then the typical desert coolness returns.

Nevada summer: Get out the beach gear. It's playtime. Watch out for that tricky old sun early on, or you'll be a true Nevada redneck. Or worse, red all over. Honeysuckle rose, sand between your toes. There they are folks, the beaches swarming with sun worshipers, a sky thick with the playing gear of the outdoor people.

Nevada summer: picnics and lawn parties; a renewal of the outdoor ritual called barbecue. Praise the Lord and pass the hot dogs, hamburgers and beans. The joyous yelps of the kids who won the war: "This is our raft, and nobody else's."

Such a nice time of the Nevada year. Time of swimsuits and thousands of people on the move, each searching out a special pleasure. Time of the hospitable Nevada sun, embracing all who wish to play. Time for new or renewed adventure. Family time, friendship time, fun time.

Nevadans, start your vacation engines. Summer is here. Yours to savor and to treasure.

Autumn

ANOTHER GORGEOUS and unforgettable Nevada summer is being bumped aside, to be misplaced forever on your personal Island of Vagrant Memory. The gaggle of tanned human hides has at last reluctantly shifted off the cooling beaches of Lahontan and Pyramid and Tahoe and you can see the sand again for the absence of barely covered skin. Debris left by untidy visitors is carted from view. Swimsuits are stashed for another season, lost beach towels are only briefly lamented and the hoisted boats are having their bottoms cleansed. Those who are timid of either the big crowds or the hottest months, or both, now venture forth to uncongested lakeshores, thankful that at last the visiting hordes have sought happiness elsewhere. The dream that this would be an unending summer is put into dry dock.

Now, those who treasure our territory because it yields four distinct seasons can bask in anticipation. We are awash in the signals that Nevada's autumn cannot be too distant. No sooner are the depleted vats of Sea & Ski lotion locked away than the final crop of alfalfa is flogged and baled. Soon the tired machines will be wheeled in for a long winter's nap. The haying crews' appetites will diminish, but only a little. Hearts of Gold cantaloupes will grow sweeter in Fallon, or so the legend goes, and that's close to the truth. The doves are in the air now as they sense that hunters can be injurious to their health.

Summer is almost deader than next season's unlucky duck and goose. The sun is losing its daytime vigor and isn't showing itself to us until past 6:30 A.M. The World Series can't be far away.

Summer's had its fling. Labor Day was invented years ago as a legal reason to avoid a day's work and that holiday has come and gone, followed by the surest autumn sign, the start of school, that lengthy response to a tired mother's prayer. Now the tiredness is passed back to teacher for fall, winter and spring. Wary new school

7

bus drivers learn fast that they need more skills than steering. We begin again to abide by school zone limits. Can anything be tastier than the school lunch menu?

Autumn in Nevada's air: the blitz of wedding stories now beyond the peak and dwindling; the fresh proliferation of flashing motel vacancy signs, still beckoning long after dark; the "Marryin' Sams," now pacing more anxiously in their plastic chapels; the small-casino operators tightening the economic screws and the big profit barons doing likewise.

Autumn. Is it my imagination, or isn't the traffic volume down and aren't the drivers sweating less and swearing less? Soon the Truckee won't be a river, and hardly a trickle and, altogether now, let the Indians successfully dance for rain amid our snow prayers. Autumn just around the bend. A new nip in the early morning air and the sharper temperature decline after sundown.

Breezes remain gentle, but there is enough zest to tug leaves away from their moorings. Flowers are rearing their beautiful heads a bit more slowly these September mornings.

There it is, that early hint of fall color that soon is to go to oranges, yellows, red, violets, golds and dabs of purple here and there.

Nature is about to change to a new uniform. The red, red robin, such a regular visitor since May, has been pulling a disappearing act lately. The animals—our feathered friends, grown chubby during summer—are now in shape to survive the lean times. Get ready for the sweet honk of the honkers departing this scene.

Autumn reaffirms that everything changes except discos. Autumn is old experiences come back to us, fresh again. Down with total water consumption and out with the rakes; the hills all around retreating to brown; the Idlewild and Virginia Lake crowds shifting down to a tolerable few; the desert, ageless, begins resting up for spring. Soon the aspen on the Sierra will glow again; the rattlesnakes will retreat from their rocks; we will cut the lawn less and then, happily, not at all.

As a Holy Author poises to give us again one of His autumn magic shows, the flies and the mosquitoes are vanquished by the hints of the new season; we turn the heat up more frequently and lament the cost of fuel and power with newfound fervor.

The voice of Howard Cosell, part announcer, part huckster, all showman, slugs our ears. Once in a while Frank Gifford inserts a word in edgewise. Autumn and football, inseparable American companions, arrive concurrently.

In these parts, announcers Jim Stone and Don Manoukian chant the language of fall above Mackay Stadium; there comes a new season of colliding young men, mauling one another over 100 yards of turf. Hail to Our Sturdy Men, Loyal and True, March, March on Down the Field, Old Silver and Blue.

Autumn. Let's hear it for the Huskies and the Miners, the Tigers, the Colts, Senators, the Railroaders.

Let's hear it for falling leaves, and long sleeves, and football tailgate party-goers who not only made it home safely, but cheered the winning teams; here's to the referees: may they call them all correctly this autumn; here's to the trees, getting ready for their late-year nudity act. Here's to forthcoming frost on the pumpkin, and to hot buttered rums just weeks away; here's to the summer gamblers who lost and helped keep us green, and here's to the returned scent of autumn in Nevada. Fireplaces kindled anew, fluttering leaves flying amok, families back together after summer separation.

Here's to another autumn in Nevada. Maybe the nicest time of the year. And always unforgettable.

I Do Love You

They were deeply in love, these two young people.

Isabelle Foley, the brown-haired, blue-eyed, strikingly pretty Irish girl who was barely twenty-one years old and the hardworking young man from the adjacent ranch, Joe Hennen, who was twenty-three and the son of Elko County pioneers.

Isabelle and Joe didn't know what the future might bring—they only knew for certain that they must share the future as man and wife.

By the time 1914 arrived, they had fixed their wedding date. It would be on February 14, St. Valentine's Day, a day of love.

Miss Foley wanted a church wedding. There was no Catholic church in Elko. But never mind. They would go to Salt Lake City. They boarded the train at Elko, waved good-bye to their families and friends and went east to Utah.

In Salt Lake City, in the parish house of the Cathedral of Madeleine, they became man and wife, sixty-five years ago today.

In Elko on this Valentine's Day, they quietly observe their anniversary. Their only surviving child, Marian LaVoy, has flown to Elko from Reno. This afternoon she will go with them to the Senior Center, where they'll visit friends. Then on to the Stockmen's Hotel for dinner.

Tonight they'll speak of memories, sweet and bitter.

Back in Elko County, after their beautiful two-week honeymoon in Salt Lake; young Joe taking over Pleasant Valley Ranch at the base of the Ruby Mountains, the place his father had first settled in 1868; the births of their first son, Don, in 1915, and their second, Joseph, Jr., in 1922; the death of baby Joseph, a victim of a virus, when he was twenty-two months old. Then came their last-born, daughter Marian.

Through the 1920s, building their Pleasant Valley spread into one of the premier ranches in Elko County; then the Great Depression, the devastating slump of crop and cattle prices. Beset by financial problems not of their making and beyond their control, they lost their place in 1937.

The family moved to Reno in 1938; Mr. Hennen worked for the highway department for a time; together, they operated a small trailer park and motel.

Another war. Hit at Pearl Harbor.

Their eldest son Don had married Irene Miller of Fallon in 1935. They had a son, Michael.

Don was of fighting age and he wanted to go. He enlisted.

Infantryman Hennen was killed in France on July 4, 1944. He was twenty-eight.

Isabelle and Joe Hennen returned to Elko from Reno in 1958 and have lived these last twenty years in quiet and happy retirement at their comfortable Court Street home. Daughter Marian and their five grandchildren and four great-grandchildren are sources of constant pride and the couple savors every word about them. She is eighty-six now, and he is eighty-eight, and they remain active and in reasonably good health, although she is troubled by arthritis, he by a lame leg. But their pace is brisk. Mrs. Hennen plays a mean game of bridge, does her own cooking and housekeeping and trounces husband Joe every night at canasta. He is an avid reader, a watcher of TV game shows, and in the warm weather "scrambles through his hillside, showplace garden like a mountain goat." It is said Joe Hennen knows all the best secret fishing holes on the south fork of the Humboldt River.

They are absolutely devoted to each other. Their daughter-in-law of forty-four years, Irene Hennen, of Fallon, calls them "priceless people."

Says Isabelle Hennen: "We aren't getting each other anniversary or Valentine's Day gifts. Why do we need to do that? We've got each other."

Tonight when they return from dinner, she may go to the piano and play her favorite for him: "Hawaiian Wedding Song."

"I do—love you—with all my heart."

·§·§·§·§·

Isabelle and Joseph Hennen lived to observe their seventieth wedding anniversary. He died in 1985 and she died in 1987.

Sweet Deeds

YERINGTON—Here in one of the most gentle of Nevada's hospitable cities, pleasant sanity exists in life's tempo. In this city, habit seems to quash the temptation to run. It seems that slower steps help people better savor the delicious aspects of life.

Here, it is almost as if their wise inner voices are forever whispering sweet and timely commands: love the living and those who died; help somebody; work beats sitting idle; enjoy life! Practice loving town and country.

Here, smog does not exist. Yerington, the centerpiece of a lovely valley, does not have legions of snarling drivers, yipping car horns, hordes of efficient burglars or battalions of complainers.

On a recent beautiful night, I came here over those eighty miles from Reno with Dr. Joe Crowley, the president of the University of Nevada-Reno (UNR). Dr. Joe's mission this crisp night is to talk in behalf of education, but more especially, he wishes to join in a tribute to a man and a woman.

What a perfect match-up! The honorees are decent and deserving and each respects the soil for its bounty, and worships freedom, with all its blessings. The virtues of the two are evident to Dr. Crowley. After all, he too grew up in a farm town, one in Iowa of such size as to make Yerington appear to be a small metropolis.

The man from Iowa said of the honored husband and wife that they met, married and have made a beautiful difference, and that the honorees, by their selfless, untiring aid to others, have toiled to help the people of the town to prosper.

I was invited here, as insurance man Frank McGowan had put it, to "introduce two people who need no introduction." Imagine driving 160 miles round-trip to perform an unneeded ritual! First, I had to find out who Gertrude and Jack Gallaty are and why they deserve their "man and woman of the year" honor. I tried phoning them from Reno before tonight's event. But no answer!

Let me tell you, it's a challenging task, the checking of a phantom pair. I had read the Gallatys' biographies in the weekly *Mason Valley News*. Those stories confirmed that they are truly giving persons.

I was anxious to learn more detail. But their phone went unanswered. Jack Gallaty was off massaging stepson Lynn Pursel's yard—Pursel was ill and couldn't tend it. Or Mr. Gallaty was doing repairs at the town museum; then, I later learned, he was painting the five rooms in friend Mae John's home. Instead of sticking around to answer my call, he was at his Methodist church, doctoring a sick furnace or putting a splint on a fractured fence; again, I heard he'd just left the home of Sheriff Claude Keema's widow, Neva. There, Gallaty carted off dead leaves and unwanted tree limbs.

His wife Gertrude was easily as skilled at eluding me. Never around the house. Instead, she was conducting Bible class or was off soothing someone's temporarily bruised ego. Once, I just missed connecting with her by phone—she had bustled away to raise money to help fix the nonprofit museum.

I called their friends. Drawled Texas-born Enide Johnson: "The Gallatys are precious people." The young editor Jim Sanford said that Gertrude and Jack Gallaty are the epitome of the Good Example.

So, on this night, after the audience had given Joe Crowley an ovation, I rose to give the beautiful plaques to the Gallatys. This moment was made possible by the sponsoring Yerington Kiwanis Club. I saw the Gallatys, seated at my left, their new UNR Wolf Pack Booster Club caps, blue and pretty, jauntily perched on their proud gray heads. Then I said, "They need no introduction, but Lord, how very much they deserve one!" Later, I was told they had been given the warmest, longest standing ovation ever accorded in the city of gentle persons whose habit it is to brew kettles of good deeds.

50,000 Weddings _____

Elko—Judge Ted Lunsford was a nervous wreck the first time he officiated at a wedding. His voice quavered, his knees sagged, his heart pounded.

That was back in 1958. Judge Lunsford got over his nervousness fast, and a good thing, too. Over the next twenty-four years, until his retirement December 31 as Elko Township justice of the peace, he was to marry an astounding number. More than 50,000 couples heard this well-known Nevadan pronounce them husband and wife.

Could he sense during a ceremony whether the marriage would last? "I would get a hunch on that," he said. "It seemed that if they were nervous, this was a good sign. But we could never be certain. So many of the couples were from out of state and we never heard from them again."

Men were by far the more nervous. Some couples had to be virtually propped up at the altar. A few came close to fainting.

They streamed to his chambers from across the United States. Some wore the flashiest formal wear money could buy. Most dressed modestly. He often had a feeling the low-income people were going to make stronger marriages.

He would tell the really frightened ones, "Relax now; if you're not somewhat nervous, you aren't normal."

Ted Lunsford refused to marry anybody who was drunk. He would tell them, "Contracts under intoxication are no good."

A number of couples came in, left their marriage license with him and never came back. One couple came to him a total of four times in a single day, backed out each time and never did marry.

The judge and his secretaries agreed that ninety percent of those he married were dead serious about the ceremony. After the couple left, Lunsford and his aides would huddle, sharing thoughts on "whether that marriage will last."

He married them in all shapes and sizes, and widely varying ages.

The minimum was sixteen, with consent of parents; and the eldest was ninety-four and his sweet bride ninety-three.

We hear reports of people backing out of marriage at the eleventh hour, but does it truly happen? It did once as Lunsford was officiating.

The good-looking couple stood before the judge; just as he began the ceremony, the intended bride blurted, "I don't know what I'm doing! I can't marry you! Excuse me!"

She fled, her flabbergasted male friend floundering in her wake. They never returned.

The judge was once asked if he would perform a bare bosom ceremony. His reply was brief and stern: "Absolutely not!"

The majority of couples were from Nevada, Utah and Idaho. The Elko ceremony peak occurred two years ago and began dwindling afterward when Utah scrapped its five-day waiting period and blood test requirement.

He married a number of celebrities, including Ingrid Bergman's daughter Pia, who was wearing ski clothes. There wasn't any notice on that one. Pia brought no witnesses, and Lunsford had to ask two radio operators from the Elko police station to stand up for the couple.

"I don't think her marriage lasted too long," recalls Lunsford.

The judge's marrying years spanned such a long period that at the end he was marrying the children of the parents he'd married in the first place.

He married some people two and three times. One young woman stood before him a total of four times. "She finally made it," said the judge. "The last marriage 'took.'"

The standard ceremony fee in Nevada, fixed by the legislature, is $20, but the last few years, with the recession grinding away, Lunsford would charge couples $10, "because you could see they didn't have any extra money."

Lunsford has always considered marriage a solemn act, the first step of what hopefully will be a lifetime partnership.

He is convinced marriage is a great thing because "I'm so happily married myself." He and wife Gerri will observe their nineteenth wedding anniversary on April 6.

About his retirement, seventy-one-year-old Ted Lunsford says, "I've enjoyed working all my life. One has to keep busy. My wife will keep me plenty busy, don't you worry about that."

An Evening in Wellington _____

WELLINGTON—Here in a spectacularly beautiful Nevada rural setting, the cattle dine in rich fields and grow plump. Crops prosper and the people work hard and play hard.

As children are schooled and romp happily through the countryside, which is serene and safe, their parents feel the joy that exists when Big City concerns are not felt. Kid-snatchers do not prowl this territory and there is no swelling congestion of metal and flesh to harm the little people, or their elders.

If you blink, as the saying goes, downtown Wellington will be missed. But it is right on Highway 208, midway between Gardnerville and Yerington. Simply a grocery store, a bar-restaurant and little else.

I drove here to speak to the weekly Smith Valley Rotary Club meeting. It took twenty-seven minutes of alert steering to get from downtown Reno to the Mt. Rose Highway intersection, and a lot longer to reach Carson City and then Gardnerville, and then the traffic evaporated.

Now in Wellington, there is peace.

Here, I rediscover why rural Nevadans are content. Why shouldn't they be? Here, they live in a generous land that is well treated by the people. There are so many advantages here, including the vast supply of elbow and running room. The air is clear and sweet.

Dusk settled in not long after I arrived. The stars came out, peeking around the scanty cloud fluff.

It is a brisk night. There will be frost on windshields and on pumpkins when the sun returns. Glad I wore this sweater. Wonder if I ought to get rid of my necktie. Into Charlie Groso's C G Bar and Restaurant. The Rotary faces turn and handshakes and smiles are the polite way of saying "Welcome." Not a member is wearing a tie. So much for my judgment on personal attire. No matter. They make me feel at home.

There are twenty-two of them. In the half-hour before dinner is served, the bartender is panting from exertion.

These men are western men. Working men. Jeans, boots, leather vests, and spreading in front of me, a tiny sea of plaid shirts.

We attack the fried chicken, fries, salad, green beans. The young waitress lugs in new platters.

There is much talk throughout dinner. "Can't we do something about the poor television reception?" "There are 480 registered voters in Smith township, down 5 from two years ago." "Having my kids go to school here is like sending them to a private school—the teachers are great and there aren't that many kids."

Ray Jesch built a house on Del Monte Lane in Reno in the early 1960s when there was elbow room. But then Reno growth exploded. So did Ray's and his Sylvia's patience. They moved to Wellington a year ago and are building a spectacular home on a cliff overlooking the valley to the east. "Hey, Ray, when you gonna finish your home?"

"Well, maybe by Christmas. Maybe," says Jesch.

Walter Straub, forty-eight, of Smith, moved here from the San Francisco Bay Area three years ago. "Dad took me hunting and fishing in Nevada when I was a boy," he said. "We love it here. I remember when Reno was the 'smallest little city in the world.' It sure is crowded now. Reminds me of the Bay Area."

My speech is mercifully brief and then I ask, "Tell me what's on your mind. You have the great life here, but what are your concerns?"

Response was instant and unanimous. It was as though twenty-two men spoke in unison and offered the same message.

Smith High School teacher, John Weaver, forty-seven, a resident here for eighteen years, spoke first: "We are worried sick about the impact of the MX missile project." Crop duster Mike Rosachi joined: "It could mean the loss of wonderful rural Nevada as we know it." The Smith Township justice of the peace, Ernie Alpers, summarized the wisdom of the eighty years he has lived: "Water. The MX will gouge into Nevada water. When it does, we'll be sunk." Said former air force pilot Pete Moschogianis: "As much as I hate the navy—let me say MX would be more efficient, more lethal, more flexible under our oceans—not here destroying our land."

Smith grocer Austin Schroder: "I came here to escape the clutter of a previous city. MX could change all the peace and openness and independence we have. I'm afraid of it."

Thus did a small cluster of Nevadans express what thousands of their fellow Nevadans believe. These people are loyal to their flag. Yes, defense is important. But they have heard an MX price tag go from an initial $30 billion to the present talk of $100 billion.

At Wellington I hear their fears. "What will MX do to our blue skies? To our children? Why must the government ruin rural Nevada, a thing of beauty?"

The meetings ends. Each of us goes away without the answer.

Rural Postal Team _____

AUSTIN—On April 23, 1945—eleven days after the death of President Franklin D. Roosevelt—Reese Gandolfo began driving the U.S. mail to star route customers out here in central Nevada. He had a four-year government contract and he figured the job was short-term employment, at best.

This week, thirty-nine years later, seventy-one-year-old Gandolfo and his wife Elisa, sixty-four, finally gave up their long mail drive. They're retiring to their snug little home here to "enjoy the four walls around us." In nearly four full decades, driving 52,000 miles a year, wearing out seventeen pickup trucks and one sturdy Volkswagen bug, the Gandolfos drove the mail approximately 1.9 million miles.

What they endured to satisfy Nevada customer-friends would fill a book. How they wish they'd kept diaries of their adventures!

As the official postal credo goes, neither snow nor rain nor heat nor gloom of night stayed the Nevada couriers from getting the mail through. Few customers realize what these two nomadic Nevadans put up with to deliver the mail. To name a few obstacles: lousy weather; washed-out roads; crazy drivers; unimproved passageways, winding past rows of weather-beaten mailboxes.

The Gandolfos' central Nevada agenda kept them on the roads to the Berlin/Grantsville junction, to Ione, to Iowa Canyon and Boone Canyon and to the Grass Valley Ranch, where Reese spent thirty-nine consecutive Thanksgiving Day mornings.

When it all began in 1945, they had their only child, Virginia, then five. Mother Elisa stayed home raising the girl, and her husband was on the road with sacks of mail. Then and later, he lugged along ten-gallon cans of water to dampen overheated radiators. He always packed bad-weather gear. He patched crotchety tires, battled errant truck parts and, in World War II, joined millions of other civilian Americans in cursing the "worst inner tubes ever inflicted on man."

After the daughter was raised—she is Virginia Richardson, who now lives in Gardnerville and has a brood of her own—Elisa joined her husband on the mail drives.

In those thirty-nine years, they had one vacation—a six-day period in 1971. Reese did miss several months in 1983, but it was no vacation. He was recovering from a heart attack. His replacement? Elisa, of course.

Their route took them to Indian reservations; to remote places where there are no phones; along Reese River; into blizzards; through summer's burning heat and dust and into mud up to their knees.

They had a grooming rule. "Wear the oldest clothes you've got." They ate sandwiches for lunch and sometimes for dinner.

The customers along their 1,000-mile-a-week route would set their clocks by the Gandolfos. If the husband and wife didn't show at the usual hour, people knew they had encountered bad weather, or had a truck breakdown or that Reese had stopped to kill rattlesnakes. He used a sharpened old shovel as the weapon and killed a record thirty-one rattlers in 1961.

People would telephone the Gandolfos at their Austin home and have them pick up their groceries before a weekly run was begun. People would leave medical prescriptions in mailboxes and Elisa and Reese would fill them when they got back to town. The couple would summon a doctor when a rural baby's birth was imminent. Once, after a Tonopah undertaker nearly tore off the underside of his hearse on a rutted Nevada road, he told Reese, "Next time, I'll have you bring the body in," and Reese had answered, "Like hell I will."

These last two years were the worst, weather-wise. The raging Reese River knocked out dams. Washed-out roads were not passable on six occasions during the last two summers.

The Gandolfos won't miss driving in the teeth of storms and putting on chains atop 6,000-foot Ione Summit. But they'll miss seeing the beauty of interior Nevada. The crops, the wild hay, the lush alfalfa. They'll miss seeing the cattle and wildlife—Reese once counted 154 deer in a herd contentedly moving from winter to summer range.

They won't miss guys shooting rabbits from moving cars, or so-called sportsmen who "drive like crazies." But they'll miss their customers. The customers gave the Gandolfos a potluck dinner party last week.

One hundred people showed up with loving notes of thanks, beautiful beaded gifts from Indian families, some cash and a clock mounted on a plaque with the engraving: "From your many friends, 1945–84."

Was there any note or certificate from the government saluting their thirty-nine years of devoted service?

No.

Wild Nicknames

GEORGE CHARCHALIS, who grew up in Ely and is a Reno resident, was recalling the unusual nicknames of White Pine people way back when. "You ought to write a column item on this subject sometime," George suggested.

About the time I started to follow up, there came comment in the *Ely Daily Times* on the same subject.

So attention, present and former White Piners: the *Daily Times* says:

"You can claim to be a White Pine old-timer if these names bring faces to mind:

"Antler Joe, Candy Joe, Mustachio Joe, Coaldock Joe, Tire Joe and Little Joe.

"Seldom Seen Slim, Heavy Archer and Fat Pete; the Hound Dogs, Banjo Baker, Saxophone Blanche, Bugsy Moran, Dixie, Fritzie, the Professor, Dirty Steve, Donkey Murphy, Big Tommie and the Silver Queen.

"Bubbles, Peanuts, Whispering Elmer, Whiskey Bill, Whiskey Pete and Silly Willie.

"Big-Nose Tony and Tony Baloney, the Soldier, Sawmill Mac-Donald, Digger Bill, Bicycle Mary, Black Johnnie, the Growler, and Charlie, the Blum; Jumbo, Mugsy, Thimbleful Millie, Dragline Miller and Cockeyed Maimi.

"The Black Basquo, Preacher Bob, Mahogany John, Johnnie the Sheik, Bulldog, Crazy Mike and Tiger Flowers."

Italian Honor Roll ──────────────

MORE THAN 20,000 Nevadans of Italian heritage live in Greater Reno and no higher civic honor can come to any of them than to be saluted as our community's "Italian of the Year." The citation, virtuous because it goes to those who quietly and unselfishly lift humankind, is given by the Reno Italian Golf Association.

Today, I offer profiles of all past honorees.

1971: Camill Solari (1896–1976). Orphaned in Switzerland as a boy; trained as teenage house painter in Paris; arrived penniless in Reno in 1914; started a paint company in his little white stucco house. It became a great company, Solari & Sons; he painted nearly every early church in Reno—for free.

1972: Lino Del Grande. This Verdi native hardly ever met an organization he didn't join—and he lifted all; he began a forty-one year bank career as $60-a-month clerk; his Reno volunteer work was and is worth millions.

1973: Louis Lombardi. This son of a Swiss immigrant father has thrived on a staggering "help others" pace; All-America medical doctor with All-World compassion; former navy combat physician (Guam, Iwo Jima) who has insatiable concern for people; University of Nevada regent for a record thirty years.

1974: Don "Zuke" Zunini (1920–75). Nonstop champion of kids, founded All-Teen golf event in 1964, quietly paid entry fees of many low-income youngsters; the Reno optometrist's widow Jacqueline carries on his sensitive tradition.

1975: Pete Barengo. Son of Italian immigrant parents, this Reno native has a vast appetite for supporting hospitals, park development, young Nevadans; gregarious gourmet; had $10 to his name when he joined his family in developing Sierra Wine and Liquor.

1976: Ralph Menante. Incurable proponent of programs for boys and girls; pusher of teen golf and youth softball; nonstop dance king; co-owner, with Lee Besso, of Reno Vulcanizing Works.

1977: William Carano. Beloved Uncle Willy, seventy-seven, is patriarch of the widely known Carano family; at age seven, jumped aboard trains to peddle the *Reno Gazette;* former journeyman baker; behind-scenes influence on youth causes; owns land on which Eldorado Hotel and Casino sits.

1978: retired Washoe district judge John Gabrielli. Son of Italian immigrants; has given a lifetime of honor and dignity to the Reno Italian community; so respected he never had to face a reelection opponent in twenty-two years on the bench; wouldn't yield to prejudice or emotion; wife Lillian is a powerful helpmate in translating and shaping legal documents for Italians in need.

1979: Edwin Gianotti. Onetime teenage railroad machinist went to war, then to UNR; mastered four languages; as vice-consul of Italy for Nevada for twelve years, he helped countless Italian Americans; this solution-oriented Sparks native is a retired First Interstate Bank trust officer.

1980: John Ferretto (1887–1983). At ninety-two, he was the eldest winner; worked immigrant dad's ranch south of Reno at the turn of the century; began steering horse-drawn freight wagons to Virginia City at age eight; remembered for an unbroken string of kind acts.

1981: Ernie Martinelli. Decisive and dynamic chairman of Security Bank of Nevada; high achiever in behalf of education, student athletes and anybody else who deserves an opportunity; Sparks neighbors had to enroll him in first grade because he couldn't speak English.

1982: Jack Reviglio. California-born do-gooder has had a love affair with Nevada since he moved here; tireless worker for Catholic Community Service and Truckee Meadows Boys Club; two-time Sierra Club president; he and brother Tom run Western Nevada Supply; neither brother has the heart to answer no to pleas for help.

1983: Albert B. Solari. Son of the 1971 winner; All-America halfback on 1943 UCLA Rose Bowl team; piloted B-29 on Pacific combat missions; survived crash-landing in Japan; his acts have profited young scholars, artists, Boys Club kids, fellow Elks and Optimists; Al Solari's sixty-fifth birthday is Tuesday. Nevada owes him a 1,000-gun salute.

1984: Virgil Aramini. Has lifelong affliction called enthusiasm; born in village near Genoa, Italy; slipped out of country with family on the last free boat before Hitler attacked Poland in 1939; honored many times for championing a myriad of causes.

1985: Larry Devincenzi. Founder of Columbus Day celebration, later renamed Italian Golf Association, that has helped so many; possesses huge, creative talent for doing the right thing.

1986: Lud Carrao. Only he can say how many people he has helped, and he's not telling; benefactor of Truckee Meadows Boys Club and many other noble causes.

Truckee Treasures _____

IN THE SUMMER OF 1976, three Reno men climbed into wet suits and began dredging the Truckee River at the downtown bridges, to find what they could find. In the beginning, it was merely a hobby for Darrell Garman, Walt Dulaney and Jerry Felesina. A wet and different way to idle away a Sunday; a casual method of capturing the curious gawks of passersby. Judy Garman thought husband Darrell a bit crazy. But only at first.

Now, much of what the men extracted from the Truckee is being shown in a Washoe County Library exhibit. The show is so popular, it's been held over through November. Inside the glass cases are memorabilia, trivia and physical testimony that some undying love does die.

See what Darrell and Walt and Jerry found:

Tie clasps, a Southern Pacific Company padlock, a Harrah's Club lucky token, screwdrivers, cuff links and a hot-metal Linotype matrix.

And 250 pounds of pennies, some as green as the roof of Reno City Hall; silver dollars; foreign coins from as far away as Switzerland; a dime valued at $800; one railroad spike and a beer can opener; fishing tackle and Laura F. Fooster's Harrah's check-cashing courtesy card.

The blue $1 chip from Gold Dust West; the key to Mapes Hotel room No. 316; knives, a dagger, eyeglasses, dice, and Donald H. Clark's plasticized Social Security card, 006-26–6111; two gold-capped teeth, an eyeglass case (Dr. Banks, Optometrist, Wilmington, Delaware); a St. Christopher's medal.

Empty ammunition cartridges, unexpended bullets, a plastic clothespin, men's and women's watches and the key to Mapes Hotel room No. 511; a toenail clipper; a ball and chain; nuts, bolts, screws, washers and a horseshoe.

Keys, keys, keys and more keys; a gold-plated Elks Lodge pin; a $5 gaming chip from the Horseshoe Club; earrings, a University of

Nevada-Reno tie clasp, a pair of scissors, and scores of rings found during three summers of Truckee probing; a Masonic ring valued at $250; worthless rings, diamond rings, handsome men's and women's wedding rings; a diamond ring valued by three appraisers at a Lake Tahoe swap meet at between $1,200 and $1,250.

Rings engraved "Love eternal," "Forever," "Become One."

Spark plugs, bracelets, a marble and a .45 revolver, inscribed "M. D. Wyatt, Redding, CA," and Wyatt's black holster.

Wrenches, safety pins and bus tokens from Salt Lake City, Sacramento and Denver; the plasticized driver's license of Robert Lewis Babb, listed at a Sparks address, born August 18, 1913; Mr. Babb's unsmiling face, peeking off the card—he is five-foot-nine, 185 pounds, hazel eyes—the card is valid until Mr. Babb's birthday in 1980.

A sewing thimble, teaspoons, tablespoons, buttons, a drink token from the Corner Bar ("Have one on us") and a yellow plastic name tag from the Comstock Hotel that says "I'm Bob."

Finally, a lovely gold ring with a garnet stone. The engraving says, "Love is as strong as death—1890."

SOLDIERS
AND
SAILORS

The Lasting Pain of War _____

PEARL HARBOR, HAWAII—It is a sunny, tranquil Sunday morning prior to Memorial Day, and at this great American naval port I am standing at the USS *Arizona* Memorial, the glistening white shrine erected in tribute to men who died for our country.

The memorial is berthed eternally off the southeastern edge of Ford Island. Directly beneath us is the sunken USS *Arizona,* once one of the world's great battleships, but now rusted and rotting in the grave it was sent to more than thirty-eight years ago.

I am among scores of tourists here. The only sounds are quiet voices, the hum of cameras and the gentle beat of the Pacific waves.

In the minds of those of us who are older are the memories of December 7, 1941.

I gaze up at the names chiseled into the marble. Nine long columns of the dead *Arizona* shipmates, 1,177 names in all.

My thoughts rivet on one name. I find the Nevadan who was only eighteen years old: R. W. Weaver. One of the first Nevadans killed in World War II. The boy whose full story hasn't been publicly told, until now.

His full name was Richard Walter Weaver; his home was Fallon and he was the second of five sons of Marge and Ray Weaver. Dick Weaver was a happy-go-lucky kid, small in stature as he grew into his teens, a boy with a plucky sense of humor and a big grin to match.

In 1940, after a falling-out with a high school coach, Dick had a thought: Congress had enacted a law that seventeen-year-olds could join the military with their parents' consent. He wanted the navy and Marge and Ray had said, "Yes, we'll sign for you, if that's what you want."

A navy recruiter drove to Fallon from Reno and Weaver enlisted on November 27, 1940, and went to San Diego for training. He was home again on a leave the following February when a tragedy in the Weaver family occurred. His eldest brother Harry, eighteen and a high school senior, died in a car accident on a rural Fallon road. Dick's leave was extended for the funeral. On February 20, 1941, his parents drove him to Reno; he boarded the train to San Francisco and the next day he was assigned to his permanent ship, the USS *Arizona*.

The legendary battleship steamed to Pearl Harbor and young crewman Weaver sent a stream of letters home. He was happy and he was making many new friends from all parts of the United States. He was gung-ho navy. Further, Honolulu seemed more like home because each Sunday he'd be invited over by the S. B. Temple family. The Temples were former Fallon residents.

He had a girl friend, pretty Wanda Temple. It was plain that they adored each other.

Then came August 1941, a great month for Dick Weaver. News came from Fallon that he had a new baby brother, Harold "Bub" Weaver, and on August 16 Dick celebrated his eighteenth birthday. He was on the way to full-fledged manhood.

The year was winding down. Dick's letters told of military scuttlebutt—rumors that "we may be in for a fight out here."

On Sunday, December 7, 1941, Dick's parents were sitting down to lunch in Fallon. The phone rang. Their neighbor Mabel Robinson cried, "My God, the radio says the Japanese are attacking us at Pearl Harbor."

To the radio they fled. They heard names of American battleships—the *California*, the *Tennessee*, the *Oklahoma*, but, thank God, the *Arizona* wasn't mentioned. The radio reports were a blurred hodgepodge of words and the Weavers were confused. They prayed for their son's safety.

The family heard nothing. Days became weeks. Even after February 1942, when they were notified their son was missing in action, they hoped against all odds. Marge Weaver learned that USS *Arizona* survivors, most of them burn patients, had been brought to the naval hospital in San Francisco. One of them, Gene Goshen, now of Indianapolis, Indiana, was Dick Weaver's closest friend. Dick's mother was committed to learn whatever she could. She went to Goshen's bedside and he told her Dick had duty that Sunday morning. He was up early and shortly before 7 A.M. he was below deck, pouring coffee in the officers' mess. The blaring alert summoned all men to their battle stations. Dick Weaver was seen sprinting topside to his station, No. 6. It was there that the first and most lethal enemy projectiles struck. The *Arizona* sank within nine minutes. Dick Weaver is among the 1,102 sailors and marines entombed with the ship.

Marge and Ray Weaver, aged seventy-five and eighty-three, continue to live in Fallon. They have the faded Gold Star that hung in their window all those war years, and Dick's posthumously awarded Purple Heart, and they have undying memories. Their last letter from him was written on Friday, December 5, 1941. "Things look pretty bad out here, mom and dad," he wrote. "But I'll be home for Christmas to see little brother 'Bub' for the first time. It won't be long. Our transport ship leaves Pearl Harbor for San Francisco on Dec. 8."

Fallon's War Heroes _____

FALLON—There had been war talk in the newspapers and on the radio during much of 1941. Europe was aflame, Britain was threatened, the Nazi submarines already ruled the Atlantic. Now, as December came, Fallon, like the rest of America, grew increasingly edgy.

This farm town was very small—just 1,905 people in the city in the 1940 census. But percentage-wise, an inordinately large number of Fallon boys were already in service. Particularly nervous, then, were the parents of military sons. Lillie Pinger, for instance. Her husband had died earlier that year and the only family she had left were her beloved sons, Bruce and Wayne Van Voorhis: Bruce the navy flier, and the youngest, Wayne, stationed out in the Orient at a little-known place named Corregidor. Marge and Ray Weaver's son, Dick, just turned eighteen, was a crewman on a battleship, the USS *Arizona,* based at Pearl Harbor.

The little town and the rest of the world got the news on Sunday, December 7, 1941. In Fallon, Mabel Robinson heard it on the radio and hurried next door to tell the Weavers. By nightfall, there wasn't a soul in town who hadn't heard.

If there were many who believed America would prevail in short order, they had only to read the words of the *Fallon Eagle*'s editor, Alan Dalbey, to get a sobering perspective. In a message written simply, but with great logic and foresight, Dalbey laid it on the line: "This war is *not* something far off that cannot touch us. . . . Let no one believe victory will come easily or quickly."

Per capita, I doubt that any American city was to be touched any more brutally in this war than Fallon.

From that terrible Sunday through the next four terrible years, the list of wounded, dead and missing grew and grew.

We do not know the number of wounded, but it was high. We do know that when Fallon counted all its war dead, there were thirty-six Gold Stars hanging in the mourning families' windows. The figure becomes all the more astronomical when you consider how many from this city of fewer than two thousand were not in fighting uniform—women, and men under seventeen and older than thirty-eight, plus those excluded for essential civilian work and those who could not qualify physically.

The number of enlistments from Fallon began to swell on Monday, December 8, the day Franklin D. Roosevelt made his "date that shall live in infamy" speech to the American Congress. The Fallon farm boys were driving to Reno to sign up. Within a few months, the names of some of them would begin to trickle into the little Western Union office on Maine Street, reported as war casualties.

Adele Haas Bron, a Virginia City native, had lived in Fallon a number of years; as the Western Union representative, it fell to her to get the awful news to families. Mrs. Bron knew everyone in town; when the teletype spewed out the name of a Fallon son killed, she would call someone close to the affected family. Together, they would deliver the telegram from the war department and offer whatever comfort was possible.

The number of such tragic calls continued to increase.

At first, Dick Weaver was reported as "missing in action." He was to have left Pearl Harbor on December 8 for home and Christmas leave. But he died in the first minutes of the war as the Japanese hit the USS *Arizona* at Pearl. To this day, his father, Ray Weaver, remains bitter because the United States ignored "all the prewar signals and let the Japs take us by surprise. It was all so needless. Losing our son and those other boys."

Real people and unrealized dreams.

Tom Bafford, Bob Birke and, at the end of the alphabet, Jack Whalen. Young Merlyn Scholz, killed at Anzio in Italy short months after he asked to be drafted. Lieutenant Riley Powell, shot down in Austria. The Indian, George Dyer, a rodeo star–turned–army infantryman, dead in France sixteen months after enlistment.

Ernie Jesch, Fallon High 1937, a mechanical genius, killed in an airplane accident in Scotland. He was twenty-two.

James Cummings, Jack Evans, Ralph Ferrel, Garnett Freeman.

The Fallon student body president, Jimmy Gibbs, who had graduated from the University of Nevada with his ROTC commission, a navigator, was killed in Italy.

Dick Weaver's cousin, Ira Inman, was dead now, too. The list grew and the grief grew. Dan Solaegui went down with his tor-pedoed ship. His survivors included a four-year-old daughter. Lieu-tenant Richard Hall, an orphan, had begged for an appointment to West Point and received it, and now he was dead.

Our Veterans Day speeches, "They died to keep us free," some-times seem like clichés until you apply the human story to the names.

Little Barney Macari, Jr., an only child, a most popular boy, born to an Italian couple—how he had longed to join Alpha Tau Omega fraternity at the Reno campus! He did, but then joined the army. He was twenty when the Germans killed him in France.

Most of the first casualties had graduated from high school in the late 1930s.

They were names, later to be hand-lettered on the Lions Club's Gold Star billboard. Real people, with real dreams, who had had no prewar grudges, who had wanted to live on and on. They were so young.

The news was devastating.

Wayne Van Voorhis, victim of the Bataan death march, died of malaria in a prison camp in July 1942.

The Indian brothers Henry and James Bobb of Stillwater both lost their lives.

Sergeant Jim Smith, killed on a March day in Luzon. Mrs. Clint Pirtle, ripping open the telegram with trembling hands: "We regret to inform you your son, Sergeant Noel Pirtle, was killed Febru-ary 13 when shot down over Yugoslavia."

Mrs. James Kerr, a widow, learned that one of her ten children, George, was lost after more than fifty missions as a B-29 bomber tailgunner.

Hal Packer, George Minor, Dennis O'Rourke, also among the dead.

One of the eldest of the Fallon fighters, Walter Sanderson, was one of four brothers in combat. The infantryman died in France at age thirty-three. His friend, Don Hennen, was killed ten days ear-lier, on July 4, 1944, also in France.

Bill Schneider wrote his mother: "Don't worry. I'm as safe as if I were sitting right in your kitchen."

He was killed in August 1944.

Also killed to keep us free: Charles Jones, Johnnie Jones, Ben Morehouse.

There was another. Bruce Van Voorhis, Fallon High School,

1924, classmate of future Nevada U.S. senator Alan Bible, had graduated from the U.S. Naval Academy and won his pilot's wings in 1931. As 1943 came, and with brother Wayne dead of malaria in the Japanese prison camp, he volunteered for a dangerous mission. He was thirty-five, old for a combat pilot, but he wanted to go.

Lieutenant Commander Van Voorhis, at 2 A.M. on July 6, flew alone for 700 miles, over stormy seas on a bombing run against an enemy base in the Solomon Islands. Later, his citations suggested he had little chance of survival. Before the Japanese fire killed him, Van Voorhis had fulfilled his mission and done much more.

The Fallon boy, an excellent debater who the 1924 yearbook predicted would be "an agriculturist," was awarded his country's highest military honor. Bruce Van Voorhis's Congressional Medal of Honor hangs today at Fallon's Historical Museum. He is the only native Nevadan ever to win the medal.

Today, after four decades, Fallon people have to strain to remember names of the dead. The billboard, listing the thirty-six killed, stood for a few years on Williams Avenue, next to the courthouse. Later, someone remembers, it was taken down. Still later, recalls county assessor Paul Scholz, "I saw it; the paint and the names were peeling off." His brother Merlyn was among those killed.

Nobody knows where the Gold Star billboard is today.

Relatives of the dead are scattered. Only a few parents survive.

In this time of fresh war jitters, of tough talk, the Russians, the Libyans, the Cubans, and yes, the Americans, ought to believe what Fallon editor Dalbey wrote four decades ago: "This war is *not* something far off that cannot touch us."

Once There Was a War _____

A THURSDAY NIGHT in Reno.

Margaret and Paul O'Driscoll, wife and husband since 1947, parents of seven and now grandparents, are at home. She is doing the dinner dishes. Paul is in the family room, on his middle-aged Catholic knees, romping with a grandson. Paul, fifty-three, former Woolworth and Weinstock's executive, is a graying, blue-eyed, plump American of Irish lineage.

The phone. "It's for you, Paul. It sounds like long distance."

The voice with the Missouri twang unheard by Paul O'Driscoll for thirty-four years triggered an avalanche of memories: the U.S. Army Air Force base in southern Italy. O'Driscoll, age eighteen in 1944–45, the World War II tailgunner on their B-17, the Flying Fortress, the "Queen of the Skies."

The caller is Ransom T. Senter, who was left-waistgunner. "Paul, I'm visiting Los Angeles. There are a couple of our crew members living down here." On the phone, they joke, they relive the past, they talk of today. The conversation is long, profiting the wartime friends and the Bell system. Finally, they say good-bye.

"Margaret, we've never had a reunion of our B-17 crew. I'm flying to Los Angeles this weekend and you're going with me."

Four of the nine living crewmen have a rendezvous at the San Fernando Valley home of Bucky Rous, who was ball turret gunner: O'Driscoll, Senter, Rous and their World War II pilot, Robert Sankovich, now of Thousand Oaks, California.

They reminisce. Two wives, Margaret O'Driscoll and Mildred Rous, listen, fascinated.

The Flying Fortress. Theirs was the third and last model. A 25-ton, $250,000 prop airship with lethal armament. Today, the few surviving B-17s are relics of another era. Then, they hastened victory in Europe. The factories back home built nearly eight thousand of them. The foul weather, accidents, enemy flak and the German

38

Luftwaffe inflicted a fierce mortality rate on this great American ship and on the crews. By best historians' estimates, 60 percent of the B-17s were casualties.

O'Driscoll and his friends laugh. They cry.

They flew together nearly a year, in the 463rd Bombardment Group, and their ship, the *Purple Heart Kid,* strained, groaned and brought them to home base alive from thirty-two sorties and fifty-two bombing missions.

If it sounds corny now, it was not in 1944 and the beginning of 1945: they had brotherhood, these ten crewmen. Their average age was twenty-three, ranging from eighteen to twenty-eight-year-old Donald Reaber, the radio operator whom they called "Pop." They were Protestants, Catholics and Jews. If one failed, they might all be lost. Each time they made it back safely to Foggia, near Italy's heel, they alternately cursed and savored the rain, the mud, the cold.

It was the flying at the targets that made them a team and made them fear and loathe what they had to do.

O'Driscoll, a 190-pound teenager, was barely able to squeeze into the tail, the most vulnerable part of the B-17. Back through the catwalk, slide around the tail assembly, man the twin .50-caliber machine guns; frozen, along with the others, at altitudes of 30,000 feet. Hoping that neither the enemy nor frostbite would get them. The squadrons of fortresses, surrounded by the protective P-38 and P-51 fighter cover. O'Driscoll's January 20, 1945, entry in his wartime diary: "Hot target. I got a few gray hairs today; piece of flak came through my left window; shattered two-inch bulletproof glass. Lost oxygen mask; trying to suck on straight hose. Waistgunner Ransom T. Senter yelling over intercom, 'Tailgunner, if you can hear me, wiggle that big butt of yours.' I wiggled." Down on his Catholic knees, alive.

They thought they'd never forget the episodes, the humor, the grim void when other crews didn't make it back. But they had forgotten much, until their reunion.

The lead colonel's plane exploded in midair; pilot Sankovich put in every one of his crew for the Distinguished Flying Cross; testing their guns over the Adriatic Sea before heading for the targets; bombardier Thomas Mills gazing into his Norden bombsight; watching their 500-pound demolition bombs tumble from the B-17 underbelly; engineer James Harmon, and his Alabama drawl; the navigator, John Henney, guiding them there and back; Leo Schwartz, the

Joe College swinger from Philly, who was the copilot; the crew rejoicing when they struck near Hitler's retreat; the coldest mission, when the temperature fell to 55 below zero inside the *Purple Heart Kid*.

The mail from home—entries in O'Driscoll's diary that say, "Letter from Margaret today; God, how I miss that girl."

The crew's little Italian mascot dog. They had to destroy him when he got so sick.

They were ten young men who fought together and who came back. Nine survive. Radio operator Reaber died nine years ago of emphysema. Now they speak of a total reunion—to be held in Reno, with O'Driscoll as host. They hope that this summer all can rally—the nine of them from all parts of the country.

When they get together, all can relive how they, nine men out of millions of uniformed Americans, did their part.

When they gather, O'Driscoll will show them one of the final entries in his red-bound war diary.

"May 7, 1945. Today this damned war in Europe is over."

Purple Heart Kid _____

ONCE UPON A TIME, ten young Americans flew bombing missions over Europe in their B-17 Flying Fortress. They lived and fought together for a solid year. Their lives depended on one another. They were trained to kill and to survive. They flew through German anti-aircraft fire, dodged enemy Luftwaffe fighter planes and in their thirty-two sorties and fifty-two missions out of Foggia, Italy, they saw friends of other B-17 crews die in combat or in accidents. Aboard their own ship, the *Purple Heart Kid,* they nearly froze to death at high altitudes. They absorbed enemy fire, sometimes limped home on a wing and a prayer, but each time they made it safely.

Then in May 1945 came Victory in Europe.

The crewmen of the *Purple Heart Kid* broke up, vowing to keep in touch. They didn't. They were in their late teens or early twenties and they came home to marry, have babies, acquire mortgages and put a terrible war out of mind.

Crew reunions, first pledged when the war ended thirty-four years ago, never happened until last weekend in Reno.

Should there be anyone out there who doubts the realness and longevity of wartime friendship, let him now take back those words.

Seven of the crewmen of the *Purple Heart Kid* met at the California Avenue home of Margaret and Paul O'Driscoll, who had been the nineteen-year-old tailgunner on their B-17 during World War II. They came to Reno from across the country to relive those twelve wartime months when they were a team.

From Thousand Oaks, California, the pilot, Bob Sankovich; Ransom T. Senter, the waistgunner, of St. Louis, where he works for McDonnell-Douglass; from Agoura, California, ball turret gunner Bucky Rous, who handles costuming for movies and for television; the navigator, John Henney, now a Burlington, Wisconsin, pharmacist; Tom Mills, the bombardier, an officer with Keota, Iowa's only bank; and Jim Harmon, engineer of the crew, the quiet man who winters in Mesa, Arizona.

Only pilot Sankovich is single. All of the other crew members brought their wives.

They began to arrive Thursday and they were a team again through late Sunday.

The cameras were busy. Tape recorders got a lot of use.

O'Driscoll was the only crewman who kept a diary through that war period and it was digested over and over by men who were examining their war roots.

They missed three of the crew. Don Reaber died of emphysema. He was the crew's radio operator. A waistgunner, Lyman Threet, wrote from his work base in Panama, saying he couldn't make the trip. Copilot Leo Schwartz, who hailed from Philadelphia, could not be located.

On Friday night, they were at the O'Driscoll home enjoying camaraderie and barbecue, when the O'Driscolls' friends Carol and Everett Adams arrived with a visitor in town from the Reno National Air Races. He was Heinz Scheibe, an auto mechanic from Fremont, California.

Scheibe flew with the German Luftwaffe in the same World War theater, and at the same time, as the crew of the *Purple Heart Kid*.

There was at first uneasiness, shuffling of feet, clearing of throats. Then the former wartime enemies came together as peacetime friends.

The interchange between the onetime German pilot and the Americans grew lively. Notes were compared, combat strategy discussed. Heinz said that with the diminishing number of German pilots in the late war stages, he was sent to combat with only a few hours of training.

Finally, when it was certain the onetime adversaries were going to be friends, B-17 pilot Sankovich and Luftwaffe pilot Scheibe engaged in a spirited, friendly debate over American politics.

The time to break up arrived too soon.

At one of the final dinners over the four-day period, the O'Driscolls' twenty-three-year-old son Mark rose and toasted "that other generation, who fought to give our generation so much today." Pilot Sankovich responded with his own toast, saluting "the great youngsters of this era."

They lingered, as if saying this kind of togetherness might not occur again. Late Sunday, someone sent out for hamburgers and they stayed on at the O'Driscolls, talking for an additional three hours.

The last of the visitors, Ransom T. Senter, departed, dabbing at his eyes.

When all were gone, the O'Driscolls, weary but exhilarated, went to bed and Paul O'Driscoll lay there for an hour, playing back tapes he'd made of reunion conversations. Before he turned out the light, he told his wife, "Honey, this was just the greatest thing that could have happened."

Heinz Scheibe later dined with his friends, the Adamses, at the 19th Hole Restaurant and talked of the war and of his many friends killed. Finally he couldn't hold back anymore and he wept.

TALES
PEOPLE
HAVE
TOLD ME

The Picture of Will Rogers _____

LET ME TELL YOU a story about a picture, which was taken little more than a half-century ago, and about the two people in it.

The photograph, made with a small camera, is a bit faded now. But if you were somewhat older, you would recognize that the man was one of the most famous and beloved Americans. The little girl, peeking so shyly at him, was growing up in Alaska at the time. Today, she lives in Reno. She has six children and eight grandchildren.

The man was the wonderful humorist and social critic Will Rogers (1879–1935), beloved for his homespun humor, down-to-earth philosophy and generosity. Born in Indian Territory (now Oklahoma), he was partly of Cherokee Indian ancestry ("My ancestors may not have come over on the Mayflower, but they met 'em at the boat"). He became famous for his many talents.

Will Rogers may have been the greatest trick roper who ever lived. He first won fame while appearing in the Ziegfeld Follies in 1916; by the time his life ended, he had appeared in fifty silent movies, twenty-one talking films and on the most popular radio show in America, and had written six books. His column appeared in 350 newspapers and he had a genius for uttering remembered words—"All I know is what I read in the newspapers," and the most famous of all, "I never met a man I didn't like."

The lives of Will Rogers and the girl in the picture, Margaret Rosi Fisher, came together for only a few seconds. The date was August 14, 1935. The place was Fairbanks, Alaska. It was a Wednesday.

Margaret Rosi's parents had moved to Fairbanks in 1931 and she was eleven years old when the great Will Rogers came to town, in the company of his close friend, the famous globe-circling aviator Wiley Post. The men were embarked on an around-the-world trip in Post's plane.

They had stopped off briefly at Fairbanks and Will Rogers had

47

stood the little place on its collective ear with his shrewd and timely comments about life, current events and his trip with Wiley Post.

Summer vacation made it easy for the little girl to go to town with her mother that Wednesday. Everybody wanted to catch a glimpse of Rogers, and of pioneer flier Post, who wore a black patch over one eye.

It was midday and Rogers had finished lunch at a small restaurant. As he stepped out into the bright sunshine, he wore his trademark felt hat, with the brim tipped down, and little Margaret Rosi remembers glancing down at "the most beautiful black polished shoes I ever saw."

In that instant, a friend of the girl's mother snapped the picture.

It was among the last photographs taken of Will Rogers.

The following morning, he and Wiley Post climbed into Post's pontoon plane and flew off for Point Barrow, on the northern coast of Alaska. But not long into the flight, the engine stalled and the plane crashed. Rogers and Post were killed.

Today, Margaret Rosi Fisher works as a hostess at the Skyway Buffet at Harrah's-Reno.

It's going on fifty-one years since the picture was taken and her memory about some of the details has faded. She struggles to recall who accompanied her to town to see the famous visitors. It is difficult to remember the precise physical setting.

But as to what Will Rogers looked like, she remembers that in detail in the perspective of the child she was.

"Will Rogers was taller than Wiley Post and I remember how he tipped his hat as he greeted us, and how he smiled at me and I remember his shiny shoes. As he walked away, we trailed behind him."

Margaret Fisher took another look at her picture and said, "Oh, I've always been so very pleased that I have this photo to go along with my memories of that day."

Pearl's Friends _____

WHAT WILL Pearl Champagne always remember about that memorable Monday, March 12, 1979?

Remember it as the day that Jimmy Carter argued in Jerusalem for peace? Or that legislator Don Mello again made headlines in Carson City? That a psychic came and went in a Reno murder case? That Texas A&M played basketball in Reno? Remember that March 12 was a picture postcard sunny day? Or that Bally's stock rose two points?

Shucks no.

It was the day Pearl's friends stood behind her.

Pearl, age fifty-two, five-foot, with graying hair—Mrs. Personality—is manager of Swensen's Ice Cream Factory and Shoppe. She's British-Canadian and she has lived in Reno going on five years.

For Pearl, last Monday's work day began like doomsday.

She arrived at Swensen's early, to get set for the regular 11 A.M. opening. Two waitresses would be in at any minute.

The phone rang. Employee Pat Miller was calling to say she was tied up and couldn't come in. Pearl got to feeling uneasy.

The phone rang again. Waitress Wendy Johnson was abed with the flu.

Holy cow! Pearl's work force was down to zero, plus one. There was just her to cook, to serve customers, to man the register.

Pearl called owner Gina Cox to help out. Gina was a flu victim, too.

"No way you can open up, Pearl," said Gina.

"No way I'm not gonna try," answered Pearl.

She called a reserve waitress. No answer.

Pearl thought, "Our schoolgirl waitresses can't possibly be here until after 3 P.M. when they get out of class. Man, oh man!"

She called Homer "Andy" Anderson, a close friend, explaining the situation. "Andy can you get over here and take care of the cash register while I cook and wait on the customers?"

"Sure, Pearl, I'll be right there."

Nolen Henson, who owns a hobby shop, wandered in for his late-morning cup of coffee. "Pearl, I'll wash dishes."

Then three young adults who are about to open "Cozmos, a Private Disco," in the Kietzke Shopping Center heard the news. Caroline Wing, Nick Xalis and John Carreno became volunteer waiters.

The word of Pearl's plight spread fast.

The fifty-seat Swensen's was filling, as it is wont to do during the lunch hour.

Young Dave Fletcher, an employee at Nolen Henson's hobby shop, moved in to fill the orders for ice cream cones.

Pearl, at work over the grill, couldn't believe it. The businessmen-customers kept rallying. Customer Jerry Nickel of Jones-West Ford went to work writing up customers' orders. Charles King, a Reno contractor, came in and started helping.

The customers poured in. Among them were Joe and Mary Helen Wasser and their daughter, Helen Becker. Recalled Mrs. Wasser: "It was a riot. Everybody was stumbling over themselves, helping. They were having fun. There was great camaraderie."

Sometime between noon and 1 P.M., Sierra Pacific Power crewmen arrived, announcing they'd have to turn off the water for twenty minutes, to do some necessary work in the Kietzke Center.

"Okay, go ahead," shrugged Pearl. "We've gone this far; we'll get by."

Paul Rutherford, salesman for Nevada Food and Beverage, stopped in. "Never saw anything like it," said Rutherford. "The place was filled with customers. The volunteer-helpers were making milk shakes, wrestling with dirty dishes, and it was just great that everyone pitched in and helped."

Pearl was overcome by what they did. "All the customers, they understood, and they were patient with my 'impromptu' crew.

"It was great, it was funny—even when the milk dispenser cut loose all over three of my neophyte waiters.

"Why, we even had an earthquake amid all this—I mean an order for our Earthquake Sundae, eight scoops of ice cream and great toppings, all for $5.50, and you know, that guy sat there eating that Earthquake and he just laughed his head off, watching us work!"

Then it ended. Pearl and her spontaneous crew had done their thing together for two and a half hours. Finally, regular waitresses came on shift.

The Cozmos Disco trio, Nolen Henson, and "Andy" Anderson, and Charles and Dave and Jerry and the others gathered around Pearl Champagne and said they'd loved helping. Before they left on the Monday that Pearl will always remember, the friends who stood behind her gave her their total of $18 in tips.

Broke on a Lonely Road _____

LESTER WANN was in trouble and how well he knew it!

Here he was, driving his old car out on that lonely stretch of road between Austin and Fallon. For the first time in years, he was flat broke and, what's more, his gas tank already was perilously close to empty.

On this Sunday morning, he crept along to conserve fuel. Coming down those mountain roads on U.S. Highway 50 heading west to Fallon, he coasted to save gas.

But heck, this was the Sabbath and, after all, Fallon no doubt was loaded with Good Samaritans. Surely they would loan him gas or money to buy him enough to get him home to Lovelock.

This was to be the last lap of a 1,400-mile, four-day business trip for fifty-four-year-old Les Wann. A printer for thirty years, Wann is supervisor of the printing operation of the weekly newspaper, the *Lovelock Review-Miner.* The company also is printing a new specialty tabloid, dealing exclusively with mining news. Owner Carol Pringle has been developing a marketing strategy, trying to sell the mining publication in Nevada and in the Pacific Northwest. One of Mrs. Pringle's chief helpers to this end has been Les Wann. On the Nevada trip that was about to end, Wann had been distributing the newspaper around Nevada and acquainting potential advertisers with the publication.

The trip had been uneventful until Saturday when Wann's 1970 car grew cranky at Tonopah. The alternator was fussing and finally pooped out. Wann found a service station that would replace the part. He paid close to $100. As he set out for his next stop, his funds were dipping too low for comfort.

Later that Saturday, he made business calls in the historic mining town of Eureka. He spent the last money he had on dinner that night; since it was too late to start off for Fallon, and thence home to Lovelock, Wann elected to stay over. There wasn't any money for lodging. He snuggled down in his Falcon and slept.

It was mid-morning Sunday when Les Wann eased into Fallon. The gas gauge was on "empty." He knew he must be operating on fumes.

Even if he had a dime, which he didn't, he couldn't have called home to Lovelock to his brother, with whom he lives. They have no phone. The *Review-Miner* office is closed on Sundays.

So, Wann, remembering that when in trouble you should seek out the law, went to the Fallon police station. He explained who he is and said, "I'm broke, nearly out of gas and without credit cards or checks." He asked to borrow gas or money to buy a few gallons. The police politely explained they don't give money to stranded strangers. "You need to go to a church or the welfare office," they suggested.

Wann went to the Churchill County sheriff's office, which wasn't in the charitable loan business either. Then he found out the welfare office is always closed on Sundays.

He went to the rectory of St. Patrick's Catholic Church. He told a young priest of his plight. He asked to work for the church or borrow enough for gas to drive the fifty miles home to Lovelock.

Wann remembers the priest replying, "We do not give such help. You will have to go to the police station for that."

Frustrated and having told the priest, "I'll never give favor to another church collection plate," Wann drove around on fumes, looking for a church that was open.

The morning service had just concluded when Wann pulled up to the West Richards Street ward of the Church of Jesus Christ of the Latter Day Saints.

Wann sought out a bishop and told his predicament.

"Are you LDS?" the church official asked.

"No."

"What faith are you?"

"I'm a Jew. Converted eight years ago. But where do you find a rabbi in Fallon?"

"I'm sorry, but we only help our own," said the bishop.

The churchman offered to take up a collection for Wann, who reacted: "Look, I'm no charity case. I told you I'll work or, if you prefer, borrow and pay you back tomorrow."

The LDS official replied, "If you wish to wait two or three hours, I'll take this matter up with others in the church."

Wann explained, "I could starve in the meantime." He left, carrying with him the certain knowledge that Christ had not questioned the multitudes about their church affiliations.

Again Wann was at the Fallon police station, asking advice. First he had some advice for the police: "Don't send people to the churches for help. There is no help there."

The police suggested he visit casinos along the west side of Maine Street. "Sometimes they have contract work for two or three hours."

Wann walked around the corner to the Fallon Nugget, but its personnel office was closed until Monday. "Why not try the Sagebrush next door?" a passerby suggested.

Paul McCuskey, sixty, has practiced dentistry in Fallon for the last thirty-five years and a year and a half ago he added a new venture, purchasing the Sagebrush Casino Restaurant. He remembers getting his gaming license from then state gaming chief Harry Reid and Reid saying, "I hope this casino business doesn't shake your faith in people." It hasn't.

On the Sunday about which I write, McCuskey was approached by a man neatly dressed in slacks and sport coat. The stranger identified himself and McCuskey extended a hand. "Can I help you, sir?"

As McCuskey listened, he looked in Wann's eyes and "instinct told me I was dealing with a straight guy."

"What do you need?"

"Oh, $10 will do me, sir. I want to work for it."

McCuskey had Wann sign an IOU and handed him a $20 bill.

Les Wann drove out of Fallon, his fuel tank refurbished, munching on pecan rolls and drinking from the milk carton he'd bought at Safeway. En route home to Lovelock, he thought, "God is still alive and well, even if He has taken up residence in the casinos."

The following day in Fallon a man approached Paul McCuskey.

"Hello, sir, I'm Les Wann's brother, Don. Les deeply appreciates your trust. He's working today and sent me over from Lovelock with this."

It was a $20 bill.

Christmas Miracle _____

ROSE DEVINE'S eyes grow moist as she tells of the family's Christmas miracle.

By all odds, Sam shouldn't be all snuggly and warm and safe at home this Christmas Day. He should be dead, a victim of last week's major snowstorm.

The big black Labrador came to the Dennis Devine family in Sparks in 1962, when he was a puppy. Now, Sam is nearly 17 years old—or 119 by human standards—and he has turned gray and he is slow afoot and deaf.

A week ago, Rose fed old Sam his dinner and, by custom, unlatched the back gate. Out went Sam to take his brief leave. He had always unfailingly returned home by nightfall. But this time, he didn't.

Morning came, bitter cold. No Sam.

A search started in the north Sparks neighborhood. No Sam.

That afternoon, it began to snow, lightly at first, then thick and wet. It was freezing and blowing. No Sam.

A neighbor friend, Dorothy Grupcynski, said, "If you find Sam alive, it'll be your Christmas miracle."

Late in the day, Rose made the long-distance call she'd been dreading. Husband Dennis was up in northern Nevada, at Valmy, on assignment there with Sierra Pacific Power Company. Rose explained the details to her usually unflappable husband.

She heard that unmistakable catch in his throat as he responded, "Keep looking."

The following morning. No Sam. Rose Devine dropped off five-year-old daughter Danielle at Rose's parents, the Orval Grundys, and went on to her secretarial job at Security National Bank of Nevada.

Her father headed for the Devine home to search.

Orval Grundy remembered that old Sam liked to wander near the

Orr Ditch, 200 yards from the Devine home. He headed up that way in the blowing snow, crying out for the deaf dog.

It was late morning now and Grundy got up to the frozen ditch. There, from the willows and tules came the low cry, a feeble whimper. Sam was down in a hole, trapped and weak from his escape efforts, muddy and covered with snow.

Grundy went back to the Devine home, fetched a wheelbarrow and somehow pulled the 90-pound Sam free and laid him on the wheelbarrow. Back home to the garage.

A call went to daughter Rose at work. "I found Sam."

By the time Rose Devine got home, the neighbors had rallied. They met her car. Together they went into the garage.

There was Sam, half-frozen, weakened, too near gone to stand. As Rose and a neighbor entered, Sam looked up and whimpered and those big black eyes came to life. The people patted and loved him, scratched his ears, aimed the warm hair dryer at him and covered him with blankets.

Sam's tail twitched. He was home again. He was going to be all right.

Reno Visitors Center _____

THINGS ARE NEVER DULL at the Visitors Center of the Greater Reno-Sparks Chamber of Commerce.

The staff of the center, located on the lower level at 135 N. Sierra Street, juggles a gaggle of incoming telephone calls. Mail volume approaches 500 letters a month. The walk-in traffic can get brisk, and sometimes tipsy.

The lady in charge is visitors desk coordinator Jacqueline Herrmann. She has manned the position two years. She is a slender five-foot-three and has brown eyes, with silver in her hair, "some of which I spray in there myself." She is a frank and witty person. When I asked if I might give her age, she answered, "No. Go climb a tree."

Anyway, to hear Jacqueline Herrmann tell it, a lot of the incoming letters and calls are routine and usually fall into two categories: people considering relocating to Reno or Sparks and people who plan to visit.

People want to know about living accommodations, schools, shopping areas, costs. They ask for information on churches, banks, the weather. They're curious about how to get married or how to get unhitched.

A few writers forecast the future—one not long ago said Jesus Christ will be returning in April 1985. Calls are not always routine. One gentleman rang up the desk on a late afternoon and told Herrmann, "If you'll be there awhile, I'll come right over and marry you." A woman called long-distance. She wondered if she kept a diary of personal expenses during her forthcoming trip to Reno, "Would the Chamber of Commerce reimburse me?"

Recently, an out-of-state man sent Herrmann and colleagues a shopping list. He wanted somebody to fetch him a bunch of clothes. He listed all his sizes, including the trouser leg inseam length. His final command to Hermann: "Please send the clothes to me COD."

One Saturday came a long-distance call from a man who identified himself as a leader of a Boy Scout troop. He said someone had recommended he take his scouts on an encampment at a place called Mustang Ranch. He was quickly convinced that Mustang isn't the type of place to write home to the folks about.

Some of the mail is in other languages—one came the other day from Tahiti, written in French. Herrmann could make out only two words—matrimony and divorce.

Staffers have a smattering of knowledge of foreign languages and usually figure out the message. Perhaps eighty percent of calls to the visitors center are long-distance, including one from a man three days ago who wanted to know where he could secure ten camels so "I can start my own camel race." Staff member Dottie Boatwright put him in touch with the fellow who runs the Virginia City camel sprints.

Mail from abroad is heaviest from Italy, France and Japan.

Many writers and callers check in, asking how to track down missing relatives.

There is much fascination about prostitution: a letter the other day asked if prostitutes are "available in Reno" and "if not, why not?"

One inquiry: "How do I become a prostitute? How much does a license for a prostitute cost? How long must a prostitute practice before she can be considered a professional? After I am licensed, how many 'houses' may I practice in? What kind of income can I anticipate? If you can't help me with the answers, who can?" Herrmann answered that prostitution is illegal in Reno and referred the woman to the sheriff's department for other information.

Once a man called on behalf of his wife. He wondered where "she should go to get tattooed above and below her eyes, so she'll no longer have to wear eyeliner." The staff had no answer.

The greater percentage of mail, calls and drop-in traffic is polite and is unfailingly treated in kind. The phone call volume reflects growth in the Greater Reno area—an average of 500 calls a day in recent weeks. The experienced Herrmann and her four part-time helpers can meet most challenges successfully. To them, most questions are routine: "How far is New York City?" "How much will I have to pay in customs to get this stuff home to Canada?" "What's the distance from Reno to Yellowstone National Park?"

Herrmann says a lot of couples visit the Sierra Street office and you can determine very easily who is married and who is not. "The people abusing each other are married."

One happy couple strolled in, arm in arm, last week.

The front of his T-shirt said, "I only sleep with the best."

Her T-shirt said, "I'm the best."

Ron Watson, Chamber executive vice-president, has headed the Reno-Sparks office for a year and a half and has twenty-three years' experience in Chamber management. His comment on "different" calls and/or inquiries?

"Everything seems to be based on the cycle of the moon. When it's full—watch out!"

Going, Going—Gone _____

FALLON—This oasis in the desert has produced some mighty prominent names—the great old merchant Ira Kent; and Alan Bible, the kid who went on to be U.S. senator; Mert Domonoske, current (and almost always) Fallon mayor, to name a few. But for name recognition in the town, nobody tops Willie Capucci.

Of course, one's name is bound to produce a "yes, I know him" nod, when the town is small to begin with; in the case of Capucci, it helps that he's lived all of his seventy-three years in this community; and that he's been active as athlete, entrepreneur and incurable pack rat.

Capucci seemed old to me way back when I was a lad growing up here. But Methuselah he wasn't, and isn't. He was graduated from Fallon High School in 1932, but he was still playing city league basketball well into his forties. His mellow baritone has gained him the most notoriety around western Nevada—for four decades, he has been the public address announcer at countless parades, ball games, prize fights and other events.

But without question, Willie Capucci is best known as a collector and saver of Nevada memorabilia. He grew up on a Churchill County ranch, the son of Italian immigrants Ernest and Louise Capucci. He started collecting when he was fresh out of high school, and he hasn't stopped, even now that his lifelong collection has been auctioned.

Not long ago, Capucci made a firm decision. His house was so crowded, it was getting difficult to wedge himself in, let alone admit his guests. There were the bottles he had dug out of the Virginia City earth; the booty he'd purchased at flea markets; and the antiques he so lovingly gathered over more than a half-century. The lifelong bachelor was surrounded by the mementos of Nevada's past, and his own: Depression decanters; wagon wheels; the precious Edison gramophone; beer cans; framed news articles from yesteryear; crystal; turn-of-the-century Oliver typewriters; clocks; whiskey shot glasses; photographs; statues.

Capucci's irrevocable decision was to sell almost everything. He gave his pet organization, the Churchill County Museum, first option to buy what it wanted. Almost everything else he consigned to Stremmel Auction in Sparks.

The task was massive. A total of 178 boxes of Capucci items were packed and taken to Stremmel's.

Steve Stremmel, his wife Henri, and the staff spent three weeks readying the items. There was unpacking, cleaning, sorting and arranging of materials into display form. The auction was conducted by Steve's brother, Peter Stremmel, and was played out over six-plus hours to the largest single auction crowd yet assembled at the Prater Way location—more than 300 people.

Willie Capucci watched as the possessions he loved went into other hands.

To some, it may have seemed pure junk; to others, great treasure.

The beautiful dolls; the framed bank notes went for $100; the framed $2 bills—twenty-two of them—sold for $180; the fascinating old newspaper copies drew a winning bid of $240; the Edison gramophone went for $460. Willie heard the people, strangers all, yelp with winners' excitement, or groan when they were outbid.

Sold—the Chinese sewing basket.

Sold—the pickle caster.

Sold—the Victor dog.

The top price, $1,100, was paid for an exquisite Indian basket Willie had acquired many years ago; one by one, his 464 items were snapped up.

"What am I bid for the case of hats? For this collection of Indian arrowheads? Do I hear a greater offer for Willie's collection of law enforcement badges? Here, ladies and gentlemen, we have lanterns, framed coins, twelve Chinese soup spoons, a zither, cigarette lighters."

Capucci paced and listened and remembered.

How he had bartered hard for this item and that one! How he had gathered so many stock certificates from the long-forgotten Nevada mines! The days he acquired the Victrola, the grandfather clock, the duck stamp collection!

On his auction day, Steve Stremmel reported total sales revenue of $38,000. By prearrangement between Capucci and Stremmel, $3,500 of the sum is being donated to the Churchill Museum.

The day was at an end. Capucci was dry-eyed, but only on the outside.

The voice of auctioneer Peter Stremmel at last came close to the end. Everything was going, going, going—then everything was gone.

The Golden Rule _____

LAST THURSDAY, sixteen-year-old Steve Mashni, a Wooster High School junior, was walking from his home on Locust Street to school.

A block from home, he passed the house at 537 Grand Canyon. He saw a small leather coin purse on the pavement on the driver's side of the car parked at the curb out front. Steve did not look inside the purse. He went to the home and knocked. There was no answer.

Steve walked on to school. He looked in the purse and found $82 in currency and small change. Then he told a Wooster teacher, Terri Farley, about the purse and she locked it up.

The school day ended. Young Mashni took the purse and walked back to 537 Grand Canyon. He knocked.

Bill Janney came to the door.

"Sir, did you lose anything today?"

Janney replied, "No, but my wife did. It was a small brown coin purse with probably $60 in it."

He called to his wife Judy. The youngster handed her the purse and the $82.

Judy gave him a $5 reward. Later, her husband scolded her for not giving the boy more.

Steve Mashni does not work. He gets $5 a week from his mother for lunch money at school.

The day after he found the purse he used his reward money to buy a new binder and writing paper to replace the items that were stolen from him at school.

The Little Big Fireman _____

FROM THE START of his life to now, the cards have been trickling out of a tainted deck for forty-eight-year-old George Cease. But then again, appearances can be deceiving.

He was born tiny, in Lawton, Oklahoma. He fell ill at age five with rheumatic fever and his growth was stunted. He topped out at five-foot-three, the boy-man, destined to gaze up at big guys. Sickly, he was the target of grammar school bullies and of high school punks. Never weighing more than 100 pounds, he was the butt of puns. George Cease often fought back. How he disliked tormentors! A quick right hand bloodied a ruffian's nose now and again, and his mind was quick, the better to quiet abusers.

How he ached to be a star! But he never ran for a touchdown—you can't be a Walker, Doak or Herschel, when you're the size of a whisper; how he longed to be a fireman like his brave father—but the firefighter is agile and strong, and George Cease was not.

He haunted the firehouses where his father worked in Oklahoma, Arkansas, Texas, California. George dreamed the impossible dream.

The Ceases—Mildred and Jack—moved to Reno with George, their only child, in 1958, when the lad was twenty-one. George got a job as an elevator operator at the four-story Golden Hotel on Center Street, site of today's Harrah's Reno.

He loved the work, loved the people, loved the fond attention given the little guy who always was wisecracking.

Early on the morning of April 3, 1962, minutes into his shift, he heard a hotel engineer scream, "We've got a fire in the basement!"

The little man dove at the elevator control and took it to the basement, where he saw the spreading flames licking at the bowels of the old building. George put the elevator in reverse and headed up.

Before the awful day ended, four women and two men had died in the Golden Hotel fire. Many more would have perished, but for George Cease. He defied the time-tested axiom—*In case of fire, don't use elevator.*

He stopped at each of the upper floors, rescuing people. The little guy with the hero's heart made six trips into the thickening smoke, and brought out perhaps forty men and women.

Finally overcome by smoke, he was dragged to the street. George Cease last remembered seeing the great old Reno radio broadcaster Bob Stoddard doing a live remote from the sidewalk.

Cease's heroism never made the newspapers until now, twenty-four years later.

After the Golden fire, he operated the elevator at the Mapes Hotel, kibitzing with guests and with other employees and tolerating rude dudes. He learned all the elevator jokes, including the one he liked best: "It's not the ups and downs that bother me, it's the jerks."

Celebrity riders spiced his life, especially Marilyn Monroe, who came to Reno to film *The Misfits*. One dawn, she boarded his elevator wearing only underpants and underskirt.

"Get off and go back to your room."

"Young man, do you realize who you're talking to?"

"Yes, Miss Monroe. Off! Now!"

Miss Monroe sniffed down at George and obeyed.

He became super spectator at Silver Sox baseball and Wolf Pack football games; he walked everyplace—he has never owned a car, nor does he drive; employees and customers loved him, lapping up his clean humor.

He left the Mapes in the mid-1960s and pumped gas. He was haunting Reno fire stations still.

The little fireman buff was disabled in 1975 with Pick's disease— premature aging. Today, he is forty-eight on the outside, seventy inside. There is no known cure for Pick's.

He has been in and out of Reno hospitals for the last decade.

Bible-toting George Cease inches on, convinced that one day, "The Lord is going to wipe away all our tears." A stroke in mid-January hit him on the right side. He is at Washoe Care Center in Sparks.

Not long ago, Reno fire chief Richard Minor strode into the patient's small room and gave him a plaque, honoring "George Cease, honorary fireman."

I was there with others and saw the little man with the great heart break into tears. It was his shining moment.

A Story of Romance _____

MANY PEOPLE hereabouts are acquainted with Rosemary and Jim Thompson. After all, they've lived in Reno since 1965; each is outgoing; each is active professionally and socially.

He is a development officer with the University of Nevada-Reno Foundation; for years before that, he was entertainment director of the Sparks Nugget. Rosemary was for years a mainstay on the Reno-Sparks Chamber of Commerce staff.

But not many of the Thompsons' friends know about the day they became husband and wife. It is one of the most romantic stories I've heard and it shows what a fellow can pull off if he knows how to plan. The marriage occurred twenty-six years ago this week.

Flashback: Los Angeles. Thompson and pretty brunette Rosemary had been dating for a year and a half. He managed a successful advertising agency. She worked as a ticket agent for United Airlines in an office at Hollywood and Vine. Jim Thompson's office was just around the corner in quarters shared by the "Queen for a Day" television show.

Rosemary wanted to get married. Jim stalled, but then figured, "Hey, if I don't get a move-on, I may lose this girl!" So, he devised an action plan. It took him two months to get everything set.

April 28, 1961. About 10:30 A.M., a gold Cadillac, owned by the *Queen for a Day* folks, pulls up in front of Rosemary's office. Out jumps Jim Thompson.

She is waiting on a customer. Thompson hands the startled guy a preprinted card that says, "There will be a slight delay." Thompson picks up Rosemary, who's wearing her United uniform, carries her to the waiting car and eases her into a seat.

"Let's have an early lunch," he says.

"But what about my job?"

"It's OK, darling, your boss has approved."

They arrive at Santa Monica Airport, tooling up alongside a little prop plane. The pilot, dressed like World War I hero Eddie Ricken-backer, helps them in.

The mystified Rosemary is told, "We'll fly to Fresno for lunch." Instead, the plane heads due north. Soon, the Sierra Nevada range is visible. Thompson says, "Let's do something different today! Let's get married!" She answers, "But honey, I can't. Not wearing my United uniform."

The plane lands at Carson City Airport and taxis to the end of the runway, stopping at Jim Thompson's empty car. The car motor is running.

"Let's go to the courthouse and get a license."

Instead, he drives to a motel in Carson City and takes her to a room where they are greeted by Jim Thompson's Los Angeles sec-retary, who holds up something for the stunned bride-to-be: a gorgeous white wedding gown.

Thompson excuses himself while the trembling young lady dresses for the occasion.

He says, "Why don't we just stroll around a bit and see what we can see!"

They "just happen" to stroll past the Presbyterian church. "Why don't we just peek in?" suggests Jim.

Inside the old church, the minister, marriage license in hand, waits. There, too, are Jennie and Bill Costanzo, Rosemary's parents. Tears flow.

They become man and wife in a double-ring ceremony. Jim bought the rings ahead of time.

"Why don't we find a honeymoon place at Lake Tahoe?" he sug-gests, before driving to Glenbrook. They stay a week at the home of his friend, former cowboy film star Gene Autry.

Thence back to Los Angeles to a surprise party.

The first morning she drove back to work she saw a big billboard prepared far in advance in her honor. "Rosemary, I Love You. Jim."

Tangled Web of Names _____

OH, WHAT A tangled web was woven when three Reno brothers named Wessel found their true loves and married!

It isn't that each brother—Edwin, Norman, Dale—doesn't love his wife. Or that each wife doesn't love her Edwin, her Norman, her Dale. They do. It's simply that:

Years ago, Edwin married Jo Anne Floyd of Roanoke, Virginia. Then Norman married Jo Ann Cottrell of McGill. Then Dale married Jo Ann Domenici of Yerington. Eventually, the Ely-born brothers and the three Jo Ann Wessels wound up living in the same city: Reno.

Confusion? You'd better believe it!

Mixed-up phone calls, balled-up hospital documents, bank record foul-ups, missing mail, mistaken identity, the confusion at Wessel family gatherings.

Brown-haired Jo Anne (Mrs. Edwin) had an Ely bank teller grab the checkbook from her hand—"You're not Jo Ann Wessel"—believing she was posing as red-haired Jo Ann Wessel, formerly of McGill.

Holiday dinners at Grandmother Wessel's: "Jo Ann, please help me in the kitchen." The three Jo Ann Wessels rise simultaneously.

Jo Anne, No. 1 (Edwin's wife) signed the register at a funeral service and Joe Ann No. 3 (Dale's wife) got the thank-you call from a grieving relative.

Jo Ann No. 3 enrolled at an exercise class; Husband No. 2 (Norman) enrolled in the same exercise class; the instructor thought Wife No. 3 was married to Husband No. 2.

Jo Ann No. 3 (Dale's) phoned an Ely hospital and was asked how husband Norman was feeling.

Jo Anne No. 1 was told she needed surgery by a doctor who was looking at Jo Ann No. 2's records.

There have been mix-ups of X rays, blood work and other medical tests.

A dunning phone call from a bank was made to an innocent Jo Ann, whose deposit had been put in another Jo Ann Wessel's account.

There is another Wessel brother, Gordon, also of Reno, who avoided confusion by marrying a girl named Lorna.

A fifth brother, Ted, the youngest of the Wessels, lives in Battle Mountain and married a girl named Mary.

As a matter of fact, Jo Ann Wessel No. 2's unused first name is Mary.

But that's another story.

Bertha's Diet Story _____

THE MEDIA are awash with diet stories.

Cory Farley and his band of Nevada overweighters are off and losing. Columns abound with tales of how to lose pounds. Low-calorie life now is fashionable. Rumors float—did you hear the one about the guy who got so hungry on the Cambridge diet he ate half of Cambridge?

Well, let me add a new diet story. This one's a tale of huge proportions that is carried on for pure health reasons.

The dieter in question is Bertha, the famous Asian elephant; age thirty-nine; birthplace, India; her home for the last nineteen years has been John Ascuaga's Sparks Nugget, where she has entertained thousands of Nevadans and visitors to our state. Bertha also is the largest news in Nevada parades or other special celebrations.

Bertha is of a height (just under nine feet) and age (born in 1945) that she should weigh between 8,700 and 9,000 pounds. But naughty, naughty—her girth had gotten completely out of hand. They took her over to the Calaveras Cement Company scales, just east of the Nugget, months ago. Bertha's trainer of the last year, George Kirkpatrick, weighed the big girl in at 11,000 pounds.

The overweight condition adds to a worrisome health problem. She has had rheumatoid arthritis in her front feet, detected by a Chicago veterinarian whose specialty is elephants. The problem was confirmed by Bertha's blood counts (samples are extracted from an artery behind the ear). Also—as is the case with a high percentage of captive elephants—she has infections and abscesses on the bottoms of her feet. Walking on pavement during parades doesn't help.

Veteran trainer Kirkpatrick, thirty-five, has worked with 130 elephants in his sixteen-year career with animals. He has never had one he loves or admires as much as Bertha. Says he: "She has a wonderful personality, and is the most affectionate and most intelligent elephant I've ever trained." Kirkpatrick's admiration merely reinforces his commitment to heal her.

The Kirkpatrick approach is a team effort, for his wife Bonnie has designed new footwear for Bertha to use when walking long distances. The shoes help ease pressures on the abscesses.

Since Kirkpatrick got on Bertha's case, she's been going through a significantly changed eating routine. Elephants sleep for about four hours and eat during much of the remaining twenty. She's down to about 150 pounds of hay a day. He is feeding her a lot more lettuce (eight to ten big boxes daily) and a lot less of John Ascuaga's flavorsome Mexican bread. In prediet days, Bertha would consume forty pounds of bread a day—now she's given hardly any. She is fed a supplement of high-protein grain; her former quota of 300 pounds of carrots a week has been cut in half, not because carrots are fattening but because she seemed to be losing her appetite for them. Fruits, such as apples and bananas, are given as rewards as trainer Kirkpatrick takes Bertha through her entertainment training routines.

Bertha drinks eighty gallons of water daily.

The big vegetarian has also been getting considerably more exercise at her barn a few yards west of the Nugget. Now that the weather has heated up, the trainer has her outside and moving. During the frigid holiday season, Bertha was largely inactive physically. As a result, her diet faltered. Now back intensively on the diet and getting exercise, she is losing about twenty-five pounds a week.

Bertha now weighs 10,325 pounds, down more than six hundred pounds. She still is more than a thousand pounds away from an ideal weight. Kirkpatrick reports the encouraging news that her arthritic problem is easing. He expects that attainment of ideal weight should do much to arrest the problems.

Kirkpatrick is working with an extremely valuable property. The "average" zoo elephant is valued at around $40,000. An Asian baby, born in captivity, sells for between $50,000 and $60,000. "Costs have been driven sky-high as man's encroachment diminishes the world elephant population," explains Kirkpatrick.

As to Bertha's worth? "There is no way you can establish a price for her," he says. "Bertha is unique; she's one of a kind."

THE
LIGHTER
SIDE

Good News _____

IF YOU TRULY expect to discover here today the grim details of crime and violence, failure and pathos, death or other sad conclusions, or if by chance you look to me, needing the unsavory facts regarding famine, killer storms, adultery and burglary, or if what you crave are the really awful misdeeds, such as those imposed on us by political knaves—if this is the sort of thing you pursue here— well, you must now sift through other pages. Because I haven't found any bad news lately.

Maybe it's that I've deteriorated as a detector of news to cry by, or perhaps in recent hours all our Nevada brothers and sisters and sisterettes have shucked aside wrongdoing. For the life of me, I can't cook up a single negative to help taint your Sunday news menu. If my epidemic of good news continues, it will be a welcome miracle. Better wait awhile before your hopes soar high. But for now, you must be content with the dearth of the blues. In this column, I mean.

Don't misunderstand. I know so very well how some readers cherish and worship the reports of mankind's mischief. I tried diligently this day to extract from news sources just a smidgen of grime and teary blight. Oh, but for a lone tidbit of neighbor attacking neighbor, or at least a lecherous husband making off with the shapely wife across the street! But nothing. Not a whiff of scandal could I find, not a breath of vice, not even bad news of a rich man's son carting away a stolen hubcap. Whatever happened to avarice, or lying, thievery and the broken campaign vow? When all other reporting fails, I've frequently turned with good results to the old reliables—sour quotes, sexual misconduct and, in times of my real need, the stories of a wife thumping a husband, usually her own. Spouse abuse or house abuse, you name it, if it's news dirt, I can fetch it. Until today.

It was the 1940s radio commentator Gabriel Heatter who spat those words at each broadcast's onset. "Ah, there's good news tonight!" He would then rant and chant merrily on, causing us to shrink away from the crass tales of soiled social linen, mayhem, carnage and the dank political rooms out back. Astute reporter, was Mr. Heatter. He knew, despite our protests, that we insatiably craved bad news. I know this fact, too, and lord, I've tried. If but today I could satisfy our bad news need. But as I said, either I've slipped a reporting disk or there is no bad news lately.

Assorted stories of passion and gripes and lust in hearts and escaped inmates, why aren't you here when I need you? This is terrible. Awful news eludes me. Oh, Sodom and Graffiti, where art thou? Give me a lone brief item with a painful twist. How about just one itsy-bitsy story of prejudice, or a blurb about injustice or something less consequential, like a beauty queen running off with an elderly preacher.

With Reno-proper drenched for a fleeting moment with happiness, I turned to the other Nevada places. Without help from any sorrowful quarter, this might turn into Good News Sunday. My vast army for dire reports surely will summon facts to depress you. Come now, artful spies, give me your worst findings. Let the old man of keyhole journalism in on all sordid secrets.

Foiled at every turn. No rotten news, not even a sick heifer to tell about, let alone a tarnished reputation or a story of some wayside Nevada Peyton Place.

I swear my sources have tried. They probed and poked for the bad and bawdy and for those sad tales that always hasten depression. But for naught. No wife swappings at Tuscarora; as for outright sin in Verdi, there has been none as far as I know. There is not a hint of child abuse at Wabuska and nary a muck to rake at Yerington and not an inkling of misappropriated funds at Wellington. And as for my fond hope of at least a tad of scandal at Hazen—well, there is no hope. Not a whisper of sin in Goldfield. Things continue to look bright at Pizen Switch, and folks, I thought I was onto potential tragic news. Just learned a tarantula bit into a grizzled old miner at Gabbs. But wouldn't you know it, the miner's health has never been rosier. It was the tarantula that died.

Is there nothing bleak to share? Ah, how about a good old-fashioned school bond issue being thrashed by voters! Shucks, not even a fresh report of stolen Churchill melons; in Winnemucca, the potato crop is good and growing; Imlay passed another night without violence; it has been days since a Lovelock old maid was chased;

the Fernley cops continue to reap municipal riches with their cute speed traps, but this isn't bad news, especially if you are a fleeing pedestrian; I thought surely we would detect something amiss in Austin, but the town drunk is away on a sabbatical, having his liver recharged; no impeachments pending at Battle Mountain.

But just you wait. Things will go from good to catastrophic. Just hang in there.

In the meantime, get out the old Victrola. Let the good tunes roll.

Tall Tales Parents Tell _____

EXCUSES, excuses, excuses.

We begin another New Year, a year that will be fraught as always with uncertainty. But friends, of this you can be certain—parents will strive again for originality as they devise excuses for their children's absences from school.

Consider the 1978 Reno excuses, for instance. Administrators Maurice Petre, Jaculine Jones and Chester Green compiled a list of parental explanations and I report them to you just as they were written.

"Please excuse John, January 28, 29, 30, 31, 32 and 33."

"Please excuse Chris, he has an acre in his side."

"Mary could not go to school because she was bothered by very close veins."

"My son is under the doctor's care and should not take PE; please execute him."

"Lillie was absent yesterday because she had a gang over."

"Please excuse Roland from PE. He fell out of a tree yesterday and misplaced his hip."

"Chas. was playing football and he was hurt in the growing parts."

"Please excuse my daughter from missing first period; she was home watching cartoons with her father."

"Please excuse my son for missing school yesterday; his dog was having puppies and he was acting as midwife."

"Please excuse my daughter's absence yesterday; I thought it was going to snow."

"My son missed school after going to a concert, as he was too tired to get up. Why don't they schedule these on weekends?"

"My daughter missed school yesterday after lunch because she lost her stomach and had to come home."

"Dear Teachers: My son was absent last week; his father was in the hospital; his grandmother died and I am not feeling well."

(What made this one particularly intriguing is that the same excuse had been written two weeks previously.)

"Please excuse my daughter; she was administrating."

"Please excuse my daughter from 2nd period; she knows more than the teacher."

"My son was absent because he had a heart attack and had to spend so much time in the emergency room that he was too tired to come to school."

"My daughter had to stay home yesterday because the hamster was having a baby."

At Pine Middle School, one young lady is absent every other day. Reports principal Chet Green, "Every time I have called to check on her absence, her mother gives the excuse, 'She has cramps.' She is the only girl I know who has a monthly daily."

My Fingers Did Some Walking _____

MY FINGERS did some walking and I am back to you with my report.

The 1979–80 Nevada Bell Telephone Directory is great reading!

The phone numbers? Well, they do get to be a burden. But all those names! Fascinating! Shucks, I wasn't even upset when Ma Bell told me there are 16,271 names I can't read because they are unlisted. Why be greedy? I'll get by, as long as I have names, names, names.

From the first resident, Brian Aabel of Reno, to the last, C. H. Zwonechek of Winnemucca, it is the unending joy of names.

Bible, Christ, Noah, seven Moses, plus Matthew, John and Luke.

Painters, ten of them, three Brushes and two Pastels, Remington, Charles Russell and Charles Schulz.

No Jack Nicklaus, but a Lee Elder.

Four Waynes, but no John or Mad Anthony.

Edward Everett Hale, a Hamlet, two Romeos, a Shakespeare and no Juliet.

Proctors, yes, and Gamble, yes, but not a Procter and Gamble.

A Treat and not a Trick; five Nays, not a Yes. No Delilah but fifteen Sampsons and two Wears, no Tears.

Muhammad Ali, John L. Sullivan, Marciano, Joe Louis, Jack Johnson.

Our telephone directory lists Alexanders and Grahams and Bells and five Laws, one Lawyer, a Court and four Courts.

Bob Hope, no; Hope Roberts (Mrs. Sam), yes, and Harold Lloyd and George Burns, but no Gracie Allen.

There are twelve Wong numbers and one hundred thirty-five Wrights; two Winners, no Losers; thirty-nine Blacks, a hundred and forty-five Whites, one Blue, ninety-six Greens; no Yellow, but a Yellowhair; and too many Browns to count.

I count sixteen Goods and two Badirs; two Dulls and twenty-six Sharps; a Deville and Daniel Webster.

Alan Sheppard and John Glenn.

There are no Arms, eight Leggs, twelve Footes, four Heads, one Kidney, one Toews, plus four Cheeks, a Face, seven Smileys, twelve Hands, Ralph Knuckles, no Fist, but Larry Fister.

Five Priests, forty-five Bishops, eleven Popes, a bunch of Churches, three Laymans and as for a Nun, there is none. There are Parsons, three Temples, two Chapels, three Blessings, three Sundays, Saul Sabbath and Nadine Holyfield.

There are persons named Plain, Moutanos and Valley and there are five persons named Person, as well as Bernard Peoples and Bettie Peoples.

Frank B. Monroe Jr.'s wife is Marilyn Monroe. And Murl West's wife is Mae West. Bernard J.'s wife is Kate Smith.

There is nary a Friar, but one Tuck; there are two Checks and no Balance; and a Hardy, but no Laurel. There are two Nottinghams, one Sheriff, fifteen Hoods, but the new directory is Robin-less.

Count 'em: one Sun, twelve Moons and a Star; two Sly, twenty-two Wise, eight Smart and two Quick.

Lakes are twenty-one in all, with no Streams, no Rivers, no Seas, but forty-two Brooks, one Ocean and a lone Pond.

There is a Frick and no Frack and some Abbotts and Costellos.

We have Champions and DiMaggios, Jack Jensen, a Musial, Bobby Bonds, Ruth, Boudreau, Aparicio and three Jack Armstrongs.

There are Nevadans named Jack Webb, Jimmy Breslin, Steve Allen, Charles Dickens, John Hancock, Hal Holbrook and no Brigham Young, but two Joseph Smiths and a Prophet.

Eleven Washingtons, two Lincolns, Jeff Davis, a trio of Tafts, seven Clevelands, five McKinleys, Woodrow Wilson, many Hardings, a Coolidge, a Truman, numerous Nixons, a fleet of Fords and John Quincy Adams, who is a pharmacist in Carson City, descended from the original John Q.

I find ten Princes, ninety-four Kings, two Queens, two Royals, six Royles, five Castles, with but a single Crown among them. The Shah, first name Dinesh, lives in Reno.

There is John Paul Jones, a Dave(y) Jones, Mr. Locker and one Sailors.

There is Sam Clemens, a Tom Sawyer and an H. Finn. Jack Pershing, MacArthur and Patton, Custer and Grant, Marshall and Stilwell, Wainwright and Westmoreland, Robert E. Lee, Bull and Halsey.

There is an army of Smiths, a pair of Sons.

Valentines total fourteen, Flowers number ten and there are two Hugs and one Kissig.

Gold, Diamond, Silver, Quartz (he being Roland of Schurz) and Pearl.

There are nine Robert Youngs, a Loretta Young, John Payne, Robert Taylor, Jack Jones, Tom Jones, three Beerys, but no Wallace; a Dean Martin, a J. Lewis, no Sinatras, seventeen Crosbys, including a Gary and a Bob, but alas, no Bing. The Jones people include Jennifer.

Eight are listed as Singer, there are two Carusos, one of whom is nicknamed "Crusher." A Stephen Foster lives in Reno.

There are many Butlers, but not a Rhett, and six Leighs but no Vivian, and there is a Phil Gable, but no Clark.

There are Heaters, but no Gabriel, and we have two Lowell Thomases.

Casey Jones is an architect, not an engineer.

Names, names, names. Kenny Rodgers, Kevin McCarthy, Charlie McCarthy, Daniel Moynihan, who lives at Stead; a lot of Kennedys, including Jack, Bob, Edward and Ted. Also one Smothers and five Brothers. And Olsens and Johnsons.

Johnson and Johnson. That about wraps it up.

Kay and the Snake _____

KAY HAUVER wound up her day's work at Nevada Bell, drove across town to her comfortable north Reno residence and, shortly after reaching home, walked into the bathroom.

Call it instinct, or premonition, she suddenly had a feeling she wasn't alone! She wasn't!

Kay Hauver caught a slight movement in the bathtub and stepped closer to investigate. In the next instant, always-calm Hauver let out a scream that rattled her two-bedroom home. The head of a snake rose above the bathtub drain, waving from side to side.

Hauver's cries went unheard because no one else was there at the time. She grabbed a towel and, still hollering "Go away," flailed at the snake, driving it to retreat down the drain.

Then she grabbed up the rubber drain stopper and jammed it into the drain to prevent the serpent from returning.

Hauver, forty-six, raced to her telephone, dialed sister Patricia Depaoli's Reno home and prayed for a quick answer. After two rings, sister Pat came on the line.

"Good God, get over here right away and help me. I've got a snake in my bathtub! Can you hurry? Please hurry!"

Sister Pat yelled to husband Al Depaoli. "Get over to Kay's house quick! It's a snake in her bathroom!" Depaoli sprinted to his pickup and roared off.

Hauver, relieved that help was on the way, edged her way into the bathroom, confident that the drain stopper had done its duty. It hadn't.

There was the snake's head, wavering upward again, only its larger body preventing it from coming totally up and out of the drainpipe. Perched atop the snake's waving head, just above its flicking tongue, was the drain stopper, which looked like a little bitty hat.

83

Kay Hauver, trying to decide whether to laugh or to scream, finally made up her mind.

She screamed again.

Again, she flailed at the intruder with a towel, driving it to cover. Again she "capped" the drain.

Kay Hauver stepped out of the bathroom again, closed the door, plopped a throw rug down "just in case the snake got out of the tub and decided to take a house tour."

Then she settled down to wait for the arrival of "cool, calm and collected brother-in-law Al Depaoli." She checked her watch. "He ought to be here by now." Actually it took Depaoli only thirty minutes or so to speed to the Hauver home, a period Kay Hauver remembers as "lasting more like centuries."

Finally, Depaoli pulled into the driveway. She greeted him with an update on the snake and the drain-stop "hat." Depaoli chuckled, trying to put her at ease. "Nothing to worry about, Kay. Just a little old snake in your tub."

Together they entered the bathroom, the relaxed Depaoli still laughing.

He glanced at the bathtub. No snake in sight. He chuckled, "Snake in the tub, heh, Kay!" as if senility had overtaken his sister-in-law.

"Well," she replied, "It must have known it had worn out its welcome and up and left."

Depaoli said, "Yeah," and flicked ashes into the john.

At that point, Kay Hauver saw her brother-in-law rise about twelve inches off the floor and heard him yell, "The snake's in the toilet bowl!"

Sure enough, there was the snake, about a three-footer, coiled in the water, its head flicking upward.

They stood there, eyeballing the serpent. Depaoli's hands darted out as he tried to grab the intruder. But the snake was too quick. It eluded Depaoli each time, and finally retreated from whence it came—down into the septic tank.

And that's just about all there is to tell, except that Kay Hauver did lots of checking after the frightening episode and determined that the snake was a nonpoisonous blue racer. "A relief, believe me," she says.

She subsequently wrote about the experience for an English class she is taking at Truckee Meadows Community College.

The professor didn't grade her paper, but did write "Interesting" across the face of it. He should have given her an *A* for the trauma she endured.

K. B. Rao's Stories _____

IN THE FOUR YEARS he has been international student adviser on the University of Nevada-Reno campus, India native Kanatur Bhaskara ("Please call me K. B.") Rao has been a very busy man. In the semester just ended, for instance, students from fifty-eight countries were enrolled.

Slightly built and possessed of a charming personality, Rao also is coordinator for UNR's Institute of European Studies. He's a man on the run. He also is noted for his humor. Today, let us serve up a few Raoisms.

The fifty-six-year-old Rao has done much teaching and traveling in the U.S.A., and he dearly loves Americans. But he sees us as a quaint lot, perhaps at times downright crazy.

For instance:

"See how you Americans drink tea. You make the tea hot, then put in ice to make it cold; you put in sugar to make the tea sweet, then add lemon to make it bitter. Then you say, 'Here's to you,' and drink it yourself."

Once when he was teaching English, Rao told a class taking composition: "Today you will compose an impromptu theme. You have fifty minutes in which to focus on four topics: religion, royalty, romance and mystery. You may now begin."

A few minutes later, Rao noticed that one student apparently had completed the assignment, for he had put down his pen and was gazing out the window, a contented smile on his face.

Rao went to him. "Perhaps you do not understand my instructions. Merely write on religion, royalty, romance and mystery. You have forty-five minutes left."

"Oh, I've finished, Dr. Rao," said the student. The instructor couldn't believe such a weighty assignment could be polished off so quickly. He took the student's paper and read the ten-word theme: "Good God," cried the queen, "I'm pregnant! Who did it?"

The Incredible Shrinking Bob _____

BOB CASHELL, the Boomtown Hotel and Casino proprietor and University of Nevada System regent chairman, is prancing around town, showing off his new slenderella profile, causing envious grief among us remaining fatties. A smug fellow now, proud that there's less left of him.

Going back in time:

If he was a seven-footer, Bob Cashell could have looked fit as a fiddle lugging around those ponderous 232 pounds. But he isn't seven-foot. The guy has to stretch to his tippy toes to even make five-foot-ten. At 232 pounds, he was so round and unfirm.

Well, he finally got—if you'll pardon the expression—fed up with himself for being so broad-beamed. He came to his senses right after the calorie-laden holidays. Too much haunch, too much paunch. Heavy load in the jowls. Cashell said to himself, "Self, you're forty years old now and you're a mess." Then he added in his native Texas twang, "Self, things cain't go on this way!"

So, Cashell removed himself from Reno and got his big body down to La Costa, a half-hour north of San Diego, enrolling himself at La Costa's famous fat farm. Boomtown aide Ed Allison, once athletically trim, but grown thicker of late, accompanied him.

Expensive fat farm, this La Costa. From $90 to $120 a day, depending on individual wishes. "But a lot more costly to my health if I don't get this lard off," Cashell thought.

First day. Roly-poly Cashell and Big Allison sign in. The registration lady says, "You fellows be sure and come to the cocktail party tonight." Cocktails! Maybe this'll be a "fun" fat farm, after all! So what they get is carrot juice and shrimp. Cashell loves shrimp. He is given only one.

It's a two-week grind for Robert Cashell. Allison melts weight off—after six days and an eleven-pound loss, Big Ed, by now not quite so big, returns to Reno. He no longer has to baby-sit Cashell.

Cashell remains at La Costa, starving. He offers a waitress $15 to bring him additional celery. He limps along on 800 calories a day. They serve him lamb chops the size of silver dollars. They give him cups of wine punch—one cup a day—at four calories a pop. He sweats in the gym, plays water volleyball, is wrapped in hot herb leaves or is stuck in a sweltering sauna. A guy blows a whistle and says, "Okay, everybody in the pool." He plays golf.

There is no salt, sugar, booze. Every day he slaps on a toga and a pair of shorts and moves, moves, moves. Tennis, hunger, golf, hunger.

Lots of soup means four tablespoons. Cashell tries to bribe a friend. "Cain't I just have one tablespoon of yours?"

Cashell views an in-house movie every night—stuck in the blackness to get his mind off food. One night before Ed Allison left, Cashell excused himself, went to the rest room, came back and loudly declared, "Allison, I cain't tell a lie. I just went off my diet. I ate a bar of soap."

Steam bath, body stretcher. Food cooked without butter. "Eat slowly. Chew good." Facials, massages. "Hey, the hunger pangs are lessening. These vegetables are good."

En route to graduation, Cashell is filled with profound statements: "It's the first time in my life I've eaten green beans—one at a time."

The two-week tour ends. It has been like marine boot camp. March, run, shake it, baby, move it.

"Where has all the rest of me gone!"

Cashell is a shell of his former self. Gone are four and a half inches off the waist. He's dropped twenty pounds to 212. Back in Reno, his clothes hang on him. His chin—the extra one just beneath his permanent one—has disappeared.

Fat farm magic.

He brings home sixteen (count 'em, sixteen) La Costa reducing books, costing $15 apiece. The man turns into an evangelist, passing out literature to his hapless fat pals. "Look guys, even my shadow has shrunk!"

He gloats, phoning hefty Bennet Akert, himself a fat-farm graduate who subsequently ate himself back to original thickness. "Hey, Ben, you were right; it worked!" Big Ben defines Cashell: "Martyr!"

So he is a living slenderella. So much thinner even his rings are loose.

Bob Cashell, still not satisfied he's taken off enough, will be careful about extra calories. He will return to La Costa later.

Enroll again. Sign anew for the fat-farm postgraduate course.

Pooper-Scooper ────────────────────

THERE IS AN ELDERLY Reno woman who lives in a comfortable home near the south bank of the Truckee River, that is no more than a quarter of a mile distant from Wingfield Park, and the woman is the owner of a large, gentle dog, who has been her longtime faithful companion and such a wonderful and devoted pet that a book could be written about him.

But it is best considering the scant writing space allowed me, and the brief reading time available to you, to avoid straying from the real story, which is simply that this woman customarily takes her dog on twice-a-day strolls, which can be mighty pleasant in winter, summer, spring or fall, those hikes along courtly West Court Street, or on Island Avenue along the river or in Wingfield Park itself.

To give you insight into this woman's character, it must be said that she is a law-abiding person, one who has kept herself apprised of Reno's pet pooper-scooper regulation, said that she is in total accord and compliance with same, that never, in the knowledge of her closest friends has she broken a law, either written or unwritten, during her long and interesting life.

But to return again to the chief point of this tale, it wasn't too long ago that this woman acquired an old, tattered handbag and also acquired a gadget that for lack of a better description we call a pooper-scooper tool. In preparation for taking her dog for a walk, she lined the handbag with waxed paper, deposited her pooper-scooper tool therein, snapped a leash securely on her dog's collar, stepped outside into the brisk air, guided her dog along Court Street, then hiked briefly on Island Avenue, past the Park Tower Apartments, thence across Arlington Avenue, which was filled with traffic on this weekday afternoon, then into Wingfield Park.

Thereupon the dog performed as expected, and she then took out her trusty pooper-scooper, scooped the poop, deposited it inside the old handbag, zipped the bag shut; she had just turned south, to leave the park for home, when along marched this youngish dude, a lad of only sixteen or seventeen years, slender, and she later recalled, brown-haired, a boy who, it turned out, was looking for easy prey, who walked nearer to the elderly woman, trying to appear casual, warily inspecting her dog as he came closer. Then suddenly, unexpectedly, the youngster lunged at her, clawed at the old handbag, ripped it from her grasp and took off with it, sprinting hard to escape, and I suppose you can well imagine how frightened she was, but let me just say that at that first moment she indeed was shaken and trembling, but, given the circumstances, she rather promptly pulled herself together, thanked her lucky stars she was not injured, reached down and soothed her growling dog, who would have given chase had he not been on the leash and been the captive of her firm grip. So the woman just stood there a moment before again starting for home, and then, after the fleeing purse-snatcher had vanished, it flashed into her mind, and it pleased her mightily to contemplate, what a truly unique surprise awaited that young punk when he finally paused to inspect the stolen goods, and, as this eventuality dawned on her, she smiled.

There then burst from her the longest laugh of her entire long life.

Otto's Diet

YESTERDAY MORNING, I lumbered into my podiatrist's office to get my ingrown nails clipped and hauled away.

I settled back and watched Dr. Blair Anderson minister to my toes. He was finishing up the job, sanding off a bunion here and a bump there.

My mind was drifting off to how I'd manage to lose another three pounds in two days, before driving to Woodland, California, and the medical clinic there for my quarterly weigh-in and constructive lecture about losing more.

Foot doctor Anderson spoke. "Want to hear about a diet?"

"Why, yes, of course."

"Well, this morning I put Otto on a diet."

"Otto?"

"Yes, my hunting dog, Otto."

I laughed and waited for the story.

"Well, soon I'll be taking off for Idaho to do a little bird hunting," Dr. Anderson said. "I figured I'd better take Otto to the veterinarian for a prehunt checkup. The vet told me Otto is grossly overweight. He's a big one, 115 pounds maybe, and the vet says he's got to lose at least twenty pounds."

Poor Otto, thought I. Dieting is hell; a task no hungry man or dog can enjoy.

"So, this morning we started Otto on his new program."

"How is it going?"

"Well, I filled his big dish with wholesome dog food. But I didn't put any bananas on top this time. Bananas are out. Otto isn't going to get any peaches anymore, either."

I was fascinated.

Dr. Anderson continued. "I can't say Otto is the happiest dog in our neighborhood. He misses his fruit. He really got to expecting it. He's spoiled, I guess."

"Well, I'm sorry, Doctor, but Otto will be better off."

"Yes. He was just getting too darn big for his own good."

I pulled in my own middle, which is tough to do when you're folded into a podiatrist's chair.

"Otto was unhappy about another thing this morning, but he'd better get used to it."

"What was that, doctor?"

"I took away his whole milk and used skim instead. Otto looked at me as though I was the cruelest hound dog owner in town."

I wished Dr. Anderson good luck on his Idaho hunt and said I hoped Otto again becomes one of the sleekest hunting dogs in Reno.

Then I pulled on my socks and climbed into my shoes and drove away.

I felt a renewed craving for bananas and peaches.

And whole milk.

A Rose Is a Rose

TODAY, I OFFER YOU my first and probably final report on the cases of mistaken Rose identity, cases produced by Bob Rose's career as a public official.

Ronald J. Rose, of the National Judicial College, is dark-haired, but only a faint look-alike for Democrat Bob Rose. Yet, he's been congratulated for speeches made by the lieutenant governor. This morning at 6:50, Ron Rose tiptoed from his Royal Drive home, scanned the frosty lawn for his *Journal,* and just then spotted newspaperboy Mike Ramos wheeling toward him. Young Mike handed over the paper, headlined "*List Wins,*" hesitated, then asked sympathetically, "Are you the Mr. Rose who ran for governor?" Ron Rose replied "no," as he has replied so many times before.

In Reno, Mrs. Harvey (Kitty) Rose has been asked if she's the sister of public official Rose, as has Patricia R. Rose, wife of the aforementioned Ron Rose. And Valerie Rose has been mistaken for Bob Rose's daughter and has patiently explained: "No, my father is Phil Rose, who used to be mistaken for Bob Rose until Dad started getting a lot more gray hair. Dad will cut me out of his will for saying that."

In Fallon, tall, graying, Bob Rose, fifty-nine, a salesman for Independence Realty, was been kiddingly addressed as "Governor" for months, but on his trips away from Churchill County, some have marveled, "Gosh, you don't look at all like your pictures." Says wife Dorothy: "My Bob was as good-looking as Lieutenant Governor Bob, when my Bob was that young."

In Carson City, Bob Rose, thirty, and wife Mary operate Bob's Alpine Ski Shop. For years, they've been getting long-distance calls intended for the politician. Once, when Alpine Bob's luggage was misplaced on a flight into Reno, he simply told airline employees, "My name is Bob Rose." The bags were sent to his Carson home in a limousine.

In Las Vegas, Bob Rose, fifty-two, owner of a poker school, has for months been a worker in Bob Rose's Clark County campaign headquarters. Everyone solved that identity problem, referring to him as Bob Rose No. 2.

No other Bob Rose has endured more phone calls and mail mix-ups than Robert I. Rose, of Reno, also a public official, who is a member of the State Board of Education. And his son Robert I., Jr., sixteen, hasn't escaped either. The Reno High sophomore once insisted to a persistent caller, "No, I swear my father isn't lieutenant governor."

The previously mentioned Alpine Bob Rose of Carson City once had a middle-of-the-night phone call from a woman who wanted him to arrest her husband.

But no call rivals that received by Rose Ann Rose of Reno. Mrs. Rose, sixty-five, received a call from a man who asked for Bob Rose, then inquired:

"Are you Lieutenant Governor Rose's mother?"

"No."

"Are you certain you're not his mother?"

"Sir, I am absolutely certain!" replied Rose Rose.

Then there is Pat Rose, Rose Rose's daughter. Pat Rose is the *Gazette-Journal*'s personnel coordinator.

Pat Rose was leading a group of Reno schoolchildren through the newspaper building. A teacher asked if Pat was related to Lieutenant Governor Bob Rose. Replied Pat, "No. Same flower, different bush."

A girl of about ten overheard the comment and rushed forward, screeching: "I'm Bush, I'm Bush. I'm Norma Bush."

Jordan and the Corks _____

JORDAN CROUCH, the retired Reno banking leader, a man of 10,000 speeches, one for every occasion, once committed to memory a little ditty about excessive drinking.

He intentionally garbled the delivery of said ditty, and his convoluted slurring of words and phrases grew groggier as he progressed to the body, then to the ending of the message.

Here is Crouch's speech:

"I had twelve bottles of whiskey in my cellar and my wife told me to empty the contents of each and every bottle down the sink—or else. So, I said I would empty them and proceeded with the unpleasant task.

"I withdrew the cork from the first bottle and poured the contents down the sink, with the exception of one glass, which I drank, and I then extracted the cork from the second bottle and did likewise, with the exception of one glass, which I drank. I then withdrew the cork from the third bottle and emptied the good old booze down the sink, except for a glass, which I drank. I pulled the cork from the fourth sink and poured the bottle down the glass, which I drank.

"I pulled the bottle from the cork of the next and drank one sink out of it, and poured the rest down the glass. I pulled the sink out of the next glass and poured the cork down the bottle. I pulled the next cork out of my throat and poured the sink down the bottle and drank the glass. Then I corked the sink with the glass, bottled the drink and drank the pour.

"When I had everything emptied, I steadied the house with one hand, and counted the bottles and corks and glasses with the other, and there were twenty-nine.

"To be sure, I counted them again when they came by, and I had seventy-four; and as the house came by, I counted them again and

finally I had all the houses and bottles and corks and glasses counted, except one house and one bottle, which I drank."

End of speech.

There is a modern moral to this story. If you're going to make a lucid speech, or take a safe drive, don't drink.

Infamous October ─────────────

NOW THAT NOVEMBER is here, Bob Gordon, the Gordon Seafood man, laughs uproariously about what befell him in infamous October. Now he slaps his thighs, his ample tummy shakes and mirth erupts until his tears tumble. But in October? Well, everything came up blah. October was enough to make a grown Gordon cry. He almost did.

Gordon's October trauma involved cars. Here's what happened.

He buys a new car for his wife Julianne. They drive it to San Francisco. But as they head home, it begins to rain. The car windows fog up and the fumbling Gordon can't get them unfogged. Gropes his way to Reno. Takes car to the seller, who has a logical explanation: "Why, this car wasn't programmed at the factory for heat!"

He buys himself a new car; loads it up for a hunting trip to central Nevada; the car has 166 miles on it by the time he reaches Vista, east of Sparks; there, the drive shaft falls out; careening metal breaks the windshield of hunting friend Brian Hall, who is driving just behind Gordon; poor Gordon's car is towed.

Gordon reloads hunting gear in friend Dave Leonard's truck; starts again for central Nevada; gets within twenty miles of Austin; hits freakish autumn snowstorm; runs out of gas; is towed to town.

He hires a man to make seafood deliveries; the new-hire is on the job less than two hours when he makes a turn at Moana and South Virginia, and the truck's stick shift falls off in his hand; an unlaughing Gordon chugs to the rescue. Will Gordon's problems ever cease? Not yet.

The "stick shift" driver quits; his replacement heads for Lake Tahoe with a delivery, but runs out of gas en route; it cost $385 for towing and fuel pump exam—all unnecessary. Gordon has forgotten to tell the driver he could switch to the truck's auxiliary gas tank.

Gordon hears about a truck for sale; drives to the car lot in daughter Colleen's newly refurbished Volkswagen to take a look; likes the truck; leaves the Volkswagen parked at a lot; has someone drive him home to fetch wife Julianne; they return to the lot; can't find the Volkswagen; it's been stolen. Gordon notifies police.

Days pass; the stolen car isn't found; but one night son Kyle and several Reno High School buddies are chatting in the school parking lot on Foster Drive; a friend sees a refurbished Volkswagen zip past and yells, "Hey, Kyle, isn't that your sister's car?" It is. The boys give chase and jerk two young lads from inside the hot property.

Again the police are called; the weary elder Gordon is summoned. It's sort of a Keystone Kop scene.

"Which one of you is Mr. Foster?"

"No, officer, I'm Mr. Gordon. This is Foster Drive." The police have one set of handcuffs, but there are two suspects.

The suspects are taken away, and the Gordon car is impounded as evidence. "At last," believes Gordon, "things are beginning to settle down."

The next day, Gordon, looking years older than forty, trudges down to the Reno police department with second son Dan, to retrieve the impounded car.

"That'll be $25 for the towing charge, Mr. Gordon."

Gordon, by now at the end of his unfunny October rope, explodes: "Our car is stolen, and you're going to charge *us* for towing?"

"Yes, Mr. Gordon."

Gordon, poor soul, fumes, mutters and splutters. But he hands over two bills, a $20 and a $10.

"Sorry, but we need the exact change, Mr. Gordon."

Gordon, pathetic creature, his faith in all mankind now wobbly, surrenders the $20 bill; he borrows son Dan's last $4, scrounges in his own pockets and finds three quarters. "Here," someone says, "here's another 25 cents."

October ends. Finally.

Good riddance.

PAGES FROM THE PAST

A Day of Infamy _____

TOMORROW IS THE fortieth anniversary of one of the most dramatic speeches ever made by an American.

It was on December 8, 1941, the day after the United States received an almost lethal beating at Pearl Harbor, that President Franklin Delano Roosevelt's words helped lift us. As with many famous speeches, this address was brief, covering only a few minutes. And as often occurs, the speaker was editing his remarks virtually up to delivery time. A last-minute insertion of one word—infamy—helped make the speech unforgettable to all who heard it.

I have located five Nevadans who were present in the chamber of the U.S. House of Representatives when the thirty-second president asked Congress for a declaration of war. Roosevelt's opening sentence is implanted forever in their minds: "Yesterday, December 7, 1941, a date that shall live in infamy, the United States of America was suddenly and deliberately attacked by naval and air forces of the Empire of Japan." In his original speech draft, Roosevelt had written "date that will live in world history."

Congress was beginning its holiday recess when Japan's brilliantly conceived and executed attack exploited our unreadiness in the Pacific. Roosevelt's urgent call went out: "Joint session of Congress tomorrow at noon!"

Nevada senators Patrick McCarran and Berkeley Bunker and lone congressman James Scrugham were home in Nevada when the summons came. But McCarran was said to have been sick in bed. Bunker, thwarted by the rather primitive air schedules of the day, couldn't reach Washington by noon Monday. Thus, both were among those absent when the Senate voted 82–0, for war.

Scrugham fared better. He was in Las Vegas when the devastating news was flashed to the world that Sunday. The "Colonel," as some called him, was chairman of the House's Naval Appropriations Subcommittee. He boarded a navy plane and rushed to Washington.

Five men with strong Nevada roots remember well that stirring time. Present at the Capitol that day:

Douglas Howard Trail, now of Boise, who is rural appraiser for the Idaho Tax Commission.

Dyer Jensen, Reno attorney, who is former Washoe County district attorney.

Grant Sawyer, Las Vegas attorney, former Elko County prosecutor and two-term Nevada governor.

Fran Breen, Reno attorney who for years was trustee of the Max C. Fleischmann Foundation.

David Ryan, Reno High School and University of Nevada graduate, now a Modesto, California, stockbroker.

When Jim Scrugham hurried off the navy plane, twenty-one-year-old aide Doug Trail met him. "Straight to the Capitol, Doug," Scrugham ordered. Trail sped the Packard Clipper to their destination. Scrugham said, "You park the car, then go to the Capitol basement. I'll tell security to let you in."

Moments later in the basement, Trail saw the Secret Service swarm in. They surrounded a grim man in a wheelchair who was about to deliver the "Day of Infamy" speech to a waiting world.

The Capitol was an armed camp inside and out. Amid precautions, the president, then fifty-nine years old and crippled twenty years earlier by polio, was brought to the rostrum. Grant Sawyer, then twenty-one and a law school student who worked as a $90-a-month Capitol policeman, was taken aback at the sight of Franklin Roosevelt. "It was the first time I realized how crippled he was." Sawyer and others in the packed arena saw FDR's eldest son, James, help his father from the wheelchair. Once that assistance was given, President Roosevelt was in full command.

His voice, so melodic during those famous fireside chats, was grave now. Controlled fury.

Off to the president's immediate left stood law student Fran Breen, who was nine days short of his twenty-sixth birthday.

Breen remembered, "The president was the focus of everything. But there were Vice-President Henry Wallace and House Speaker Alben Barkley, right up there close to him. I remember how absolutely jammed the chamber was." Not long afterward, *Life* magazine's cover page photograph of the event showed Fran Breen's forearms and hands, visible at the extreme right.

Dyer Jensen, twenty-one, also a law student, gained admission because he was a $60-a-month elevator operator on the Senate side of the Capitol. "All of us were searched coming in. Earlier, there had been an Orson Welles unrealness [reference to the 1938 Halloween night radio fantasy "War of the Worlds"]. But as the president spoke, it was all so real. I remember the absolute quiet. For drama, nothing I ever heard could top it."

In the great heights of Grant Sawyer's career, nothing has ever come close to the emotion he felt that day. "There was absolutely no sound as President Roosevelt spoke. It was by far the most dramatic moment of my life."

Breen recalls how dark the chamber seemed. Still photographs confirm his good memory. Trail recalls: "I had called home to Nevada the night before, and my parents told of rumors the enemy had blocked Donner Pass. Now Roosevelt's words lifted us and we got out of there knowing we were gonna lick 'em."

Within short months, four of the five young Nevadans were part of an American uniformed force ultimately numbering millions. Future governor Sawyer was with the army; navyman Dyer Jensen took part in ten Pacific battles; Doug Trail was a mountain division combat veteran in Europe; Fran Breen was with naval intelligence in both Atlantic and Pacific theaters.

The fifth Nevadan, David Ryan, was a U.S. Senate page at the time of the attack. He was then thirteen years old and was as stunned by the entry into war as any of the others.

Of Nevada's wartime congressional delegation, only Scrugham did not live to see World War II victory. He died six weeks before Japan's total surrender in August 1945.

The Men Who Built Hoover Dam ___

BOULDER CITY—Fifty years ago, when they were in their late teens or their twenties, they came here afoot or they drove rattletrap cars, hitchhiked or rode the rails. Once here, they toiled and built wondrous Hoover Dam, that mightiest of Great Depression projects that changed millions of lives for the better.

This week, a few hundred of them came back, knelt at the Altar of Nostalgia, drank the lovely nectar called remembrance and thoroughly treasured every moment of their half-century reunion.

Such a long time after they had poured that first drop of dam cement, they marched in, baldish or gray, men in their late sixties or their seventies. They came with pride, sharply dressed and most on the lean side.

They yelped like they were the teenagers of yesteryear. "Where's Frank? Anyone seen Lou? Remember that gangly electrician, Charlie? What's become of him? What's that? Joe died? I'm so very sorry."

They first came together last Saturday evening, calling out hopefully the names of the boys turned to men they'd not seen in years. Men embraced, pumped flesh, giggled, laughed and some cried. The next night at a formal dinner celebration, the scene of camaraderie was repeated, except there was an unexpected crush of celebrants. At the Union Plaza Hotel in Las Vegas they had figured on a crowd of 400. The men and their ladies kept pouring in. They swarmed over one another, flooded the bars and swapped tales of building that wonder of the world.

Through dinner and beyond they chanted stories of the past, remembering the tiniest of details. Accidents, minor and major, were called up on their memory screens. They built the dam over again in their minds.

They invoked, time and again, the name of their No. 1 leader, Frank Crowe, who was superintendent of Six Companies, Inc., general contractor of the Hoover project. Crowe, now dead, was one of the mightiest builders of dams in American history. Over and over they said, "Crowe, he was fair. Crowe, he cared. Frank Crowe was a man's man." The crowd remembered that after the Hoover job was finished in 1935, Crowe moved on, taking many of these same men with him to construct such great projects as Parker Dam in Arizona and Shasta in California. By the time his long career ended, he had built nineteen major dams.

The reunion celebrants chuckled at today's bureaucratic road-blocks. Environmental studies, red-tape capers, impact studies that seem endless. They wondered aloud if a Hoover Dam could be built efficiently, if at all, given today's monstrous government tangles. Probably not.

That Hoover was erected so efficiently, and two years ahead of schedule, was testimony to the commitment of Crowe and his loyal legions. Schedules were stuck to. Goals were met. Loafing was ta-boo. Featherbedding did not exist.

Close to 100 men, of the thousands on the 1930s payroll, died on the project. The heaviest toll came from heat prostration. Early on, many scalers of the dangerous canyon walls became casualties.

Here this week, the celebrants yelped good-natured protest every time the name "Hoover Dam" was used. "It'll always be Boulder Dam to us," they shouted. The background of that exchange: first it was called Hoover, after President Herbert Hoover. Then Franklin Roosevelt came to Boulder City on September 30, 1935, to dedi-cate the dam. His speech was written, but then interior secretary Harold Ickes struck out all the Hoover references, inserting "Boul-der" in their place. In 1947, Harry Truman got the name changed back to Hoover.

Statistically and realistically, what Hoover Dam has done for the Southwest over all these years reinforces the pride of the men who built it. Parts of Arizona and Nevada deserts flowered as a result. Water came to the parched Imperial Valley, electric power to the whole of the region. There is so much concrete in the dam that if you took it all you could build a sixteen-foot-wide highway from San Francisco to New York. Hoover generates enough power to burn 40-watt bulbs in every house in America.

Speaking of power: nothing burned hotter or brighter in America this week than the pride of those who built the dam that turned on the power in this part of our land.

The Campus Presidents Return ___

A TREMENDOUS research job and follow-through led to a "first" at the University of Nevada-Reno on commencement weekend—it was a reunion of past student body presidents.

Thanks to prodigious combing, the list is almost complete. Congratulations are especially due to Hans Wolfe, a vice-president of First Interstate Bank, himself a former UNR president. He headed the task force that tracked the elusive missing and arranged the reunion.

Wolfe's story is one of the most fascinating of the student leaders. He was born in Germany. Before World War II, he came to our free land, now his free land. Popular, gregarious, bright and ever ready to assume responsibility, Wolfe was elected to lead Nevada-Reno's postwar collegians in 1947. He was the first president to be paid. He earned $50 a month. Now they earn $400 a month.

The first president was Nathaniel Dunsdon, chosen in 1899. Two Richard Bryans served. Richard Bryan (1921), now living in Carmichael, California, is the eldest surviving leader. Nevada's present governor, Dick Bryan, lives in Carson City at 606 N. Mountain Street. He led in 1959, succeeding Donald Travis, now principal of Churchill County High School in Fallon.

There were as many as thirty-five former student presidents on the UNR quadrangle Saturday at the school's ninety-fourth commencement. Three were seated with the official party—Governor Bryan and University of Nevada System regents Frankie Sue Del Papa (1971) and Dan Klaich (1972). Others included Reno engineer Milton Sharp (1954), whose daughter Margaret Sharp ranked No. 3 in the 1984 race for the Herz gold medal; and father and son Procter Hug, Sr. (1926), and Judge Procter Hug, Jr. (1953), the grandfather and uncle of Margaret Sharp.

The list of student body presidents is a virtual Who's Who of past and present Nevadans.

The deceased (and year in office) include Seymour Case (1902); William Settlemeyer (1913); Ira Redfern (1919); Jack Walther (1931); James Eliades (1952); and Mike Ingersoll (1966). Two father-son combinations served: the Procter Hugs and the late Keith Lee (1933) and Keith L. Lee (1965), Reno lawyer.

There had not been a woman president until World War II. Ray Garamendi was in office when war began in 1941, followed by Charlie Mapes (1942). When the late Gene Mastroianni (1943) was called to combat, Dottie Savage Paterson, now deceased, succeeded him. There followed the late Helen Batjer (1944) and Leanore Hill (1945), who could not be located by Wolfe and his helpers.

The second eldest former president responding was Melvin Sanders (1923), age eighty-six, resident of Temple City, California. Mr. Sanders wrote: "I cherish having been an ASUN president. Now I am infirm—that and failing vision prevent me from joining you." He enclosed an unsolicited check for $30.

The people who dreamed up the reunion were Wolfe and William Siegel, outgoing UNR president, who graduated in engineering last Saturday.

They got heavy-duty help from Klaich, Gregory Neuweiler (1979) and Chris Polimeni, who will serve as campus leader in 1984–85, and Chuck Coyle (1957), principal of Reno's Echo Loder School.

When former presidents received invitations to the reunion, acceptances poured in. A busy schedule consumed them—a dinner at the Governor's Mansion; seating in their special section at commencement, followed by a lunch in the Lawlor Events Center.

Other former presidents attending were Harry Frost (1927); Carol Cross (1930), former crackerjack newsman, from Vallejo, California; Dr. Edwin Cantlon (1932), brother of the late student body leader Vernon Cantlon (1928); Carl Dodge (1936), Fallon rancher and former state legislative star; Reno dentist Clair Earl (1955); and prominent California cardiologist Richard Taw, Sr. (1938), of Inglewood.

The late James M. Glynn, much-decorated fighter pilot in the South Pacific theater during World War II, followed Hans Wolfe to the presidency in 1948. His widow, Marilyn Reynolds Glynn of Reno, attended weekend events.

Other returnees were Sparks assemblyman Jim Stone (1977); Las Vegas newswoman Stephanie Brown (1981); and Doc Bodensteiner (1982), now of Washington, D.C.

Sagebrush Editors' Reunion _____

TALK ABOUT YOUR Major League challenges!

Guy Clifton, sports editor of the *North Tahoe Bonanza* at Incline Village, has taken on a hefty project—organizing a reunion of former editors of the *Sagebrush,* the student newspaper at the University of Nevada-Reno.

The trick, as Clifton will quickly tell you, is finding those onetime campus newspaper leaders. He was editor of the *Sagebrush* in 1985–86. The newspaper was founded in 1893 as the *Student Record,* a name that finally was given up in favor of *Sagebrush* in 1920. The first editor, Charles Magill, served during the 1893–94 school year.

Clifton's plan is to hold a reunion on campus during the UNR Homecoming celebration next month. He talks now of broadening the ex-*Sagebrush*ers party to include all staffers, as well as editors. And that takes in a heap of a lot of folks.

The list of editors reads like a Who's Who in Nevada and other parts of the country. Here is a sampling, including the editorship year:

Fred Anderson (1927–28) became a Rhodes scholar, graduated from Harvard Medical School, served as a University of Nevada System regent for twenty-two years and lives in retirement in Reno after an outstanding career as a Nevada physician.

Joseph R. Jackson (1931–32), whose father once ran the *Sparks Tribune,* was a Mr. Everything managing editor for years at the *Reno Evening Gazette.* Jackson lives in retirement in Reno.

John Brackett (1937–38), native of Manhattan, the famous old mining camp in Nye County, who after *Nevada State Journal* duty, became editor, then publisher at the Visalia, California, *Times-Delta.*

Frank McCulloch (1940–41), a Fernley boy who became a great newspaper and *Time* magazine performer. The onetime *Reno Gazette* staffer's star quality as reporter is equaled by his skills as editor. McCulloch is now managing editor of the *San Francisco Examiner.*

Gene Evans (1947–48) was a GI who came home from the war to get his college education, former *Elko Daily Free Press* city editor and one of Reno's premier advertising agency people.

Mark Curtis (1950–51) emerged from the trauma of a prisoner of war camp to become one of Nevada's all-time public relations–advertising aces. In his many years with Harrah's, he counseled a gaggle of Harrah's executives on PR matters.

Paul Finch (1955–56), a feisty marine who survived close calls in Korea and in a long and distinguished wire service career was twice named the Associated Press "Newsman of the Year." Now with the *New York Times* syndicate and based in Los Angeles.

Warren Lerude (1959–60), long on talent, big on raw nerve and brimming with communications profession savvy, he shared a Pulitzer Prize in 1976 while executive editor of the *Reno Gazette-Journal.* Now a UNR journalism professor and co-author of the book *American Commander in Spain.*

Sig Rogich (1965–66) has become a nationally known advertising whiz, who counsels political heavyweights, including Ronald Reagan. A millionaire several times over; lives in Las Vegas.

Tom Wixon (1969–70) was co-editor with Mike Cuno. Wixon is an outstanding all-around newspaperman and clings firmly to his journalism love—writing. He is a chief reason why the *Gardnerville Record-Courier* is one of Nevada's best weekly newspapers.

Kelsie Harder (1973–74 and 1974–75) one of the few *Sagebrush*ers to serve back-to-back years as editor. Strong writer, but known more then and now for his sterling ability as artist. Chairman of the art department at Truckee Meadows Community College.

Ruth Mills (1979–80)—this is one of those stories you're hearing more and more about these days. Mills started at UNR in the 1950s, left to marry and rear her children. Then she returned to campus and got her degree. Under her editorship, the weekly *Sparks Tribune* is building into a formidable local news–oriented publication.

There are so many more, but I should mention some who are deceased. Silas Ross was editor for a record three years (1906, 1908, 1909) and those of you who've been around here awhile know he later served the university system as regent; Harvey Dondero

(1930–31) became an outstanding public school educator and died a month ago; Frank Sullivan went from the campus to the *Nevada State Journal* and a long managing editorship; Frank Johnson (1951–52) was a wonderful writer (his column the "Lighter Touch" was a most popular *Nevada State Journal* feature for years) and strong executive.

A Man and His Music _____

A STORY ABOUT Reno octogenarian Victor Vindrola, the man and his music. For a half-century, Nevadans danced to his songs. In that span, he taught hundreds to play his beloved accordion—and if he had his life to live again, you'd better believe he would chart the same career lyrics.

Vindrola came to my office last week and we zipped through an enjoyable interview. He sat across from me, his twinkling blue eyes lively, reflecting memories of Reno history, memories so vivid that events seem to him to have occurred just yesterday. He will turn eighty-one on this Valentine's Day. His pale hair is thinning. But Victor Vindrola remains young at heart and spry of step. He had a pacemaker installed last Christmas Day and it has helped him recapture energy that had waned.

It seems to him like only yesterday that he was a teenager. He lived his first sixteen years in his native Italy, then it was time to make a new life in the United States. Uncle John sent the boy $350 for passage. Victor had $2 left when he got off the train at the Southern Pacific Depot on Commercial Row in Reno on March 1, 1920. What he saw after Uncle John greeted him was small Reno, a town of low-slung buildings. Its population that census year was 12,000. The tallest building was Reno National Bank, all four stories of it; they had just got around to paving (concrete) Virginia Street. The University of Nevada to the north was a smattering of little buildings. The south city limits fell at Cheney Street and the territory beyond that was ranch property.

Vindrola worked days, washing dishes at the Toscano Hotel, earning $2 a day and room and board. Or doing chores at the Barengo Brothers' Grocery on Commercial Row. Or washing dishes at the Italia Restaurant and Saloon.

He owned a clarinet but a cousin borrowed it and hocked it. Vindrola, then seventeen and going to night school at Reno High on West Street, shopped for a substitute instrument. He fell in love with the accordion. A Reno piano player taught him the instrument's basics and helped him learn to read music and Vindrola's lifework was born. He was playing professionally by 1924. His first job, in a private home in Glendale, east of Reno proper, paid him $12.

He married Irene Pezzi and they bought the Center Street Cigar Store. She operated it from 1929 until they sold it in 1936. In the meantime, his career as professional musician soared. He competed for dance jobs with the only other two accordionists in town, Louie Rosasco and Tony Peccetti. The three became fast friends.

In the late 1920s, and early 1930s, Prohibition existed, but in Reno booze flowed and so did music. Vindrola and his musicians were in great demand. In the good old days they did gigs at such night spots as the Dog House, the Cow Shed, Lawton's Hot Springs, Reno Hot Springs, the Ship and Shed, the Ship and the Bottle; it was a pleasure to play at the Cedars Night Club, north of Virginia Lake, or at the Country Club on Plumas Street on what is now Washoe Golf Course property. Among Victor's personal favorite playing haunts were the Pagni brothers' Jubilee Club south on U.S. Highway 395 and the Vista Beer Garden, east of Sparks.

He had more than 1,000 songs in his mind at his prime and needed that mental store, for when dance music ruled, requests came from the floor and you'd better be able to satisfy the music-hungry customers.

In Depression years, the young Italian boy, once dirt poor, could earn as much as $5 for a seven-hour night. He formed his own dance group—including Webb Millan, Lee Arthur, Elva Longfield, Duane Collins and Bill Albert. As leader, Vindrola's take-home pay climbed to $10 a job.

On weekends, the Vindrola orchestra would hit the road—try Hobart Wells in northern California on a winter's night with the temperature 26 degrees below for pure survival tactics—or remote Gerlach or McDermitt. The boys roamed from Lake Tahoe (they played at Governor Fred Balzar's exclusive party there on that night in 1931 when gaming was legalized), to Tonopah and Goldfield. In fact, they played every community in Nevada except Las Vegas, Elko and Caliente. They wore out cars on Nevada's primitive roads. But they never wore out their welcome.

Through most of those years, Vindrola taught accordion by day. Fred Davis of the Reno-Sparks Chamber of Commerce was among his pupils. Vindrola no longer plays. He has been widowed since 1958.

He remains a happy man. He has his friends, his family and music memories that will always enrich him. He did miss one thing though. He was always playing music for others. In his fifty-year career, he never danced.

"Pappy"

TWELVE YEARS ago today, they put him into the earth, next to the small young tree, on the grassy slope overlooking Reno. They stood at his grave and they were happy they had known him personally. It was sad that the old man had died. Afterward, when they had gone, one could remember the flowers, mountains of flowers, sent for him from around the world. He was such an unforgettable man.

But they seldom send him flowers anymore.

Last year on Memorial Day, there was a single plastic rose. And again, as every year, the fresh-cut bouquet, put there by someone whose college education was paid for by the old man. That was all.

But forget him? Not if you knew Raymond I. "Pappy" Smith. Never.

Remember him? Yes. Especially if you were his employee during "Pappy's" heyday at Harolds Club. This week, those who had worked for him paid him tribute.

They commissioned a portrait bust of the Harolds Club's co-founder. Done by the noted Reno artist Yolande Sheppard, the bronze is a remarkable likeness of the amazing Raymond I. "Pappy" Smith.

Only yesterday: February 23, 1935. Raymond I. Smith, age forty-eight, and his sons Raymond and Harold opened a hole-in-the-wall gaming operation at 234 N. Virginia Street, on a shoe-string $2,000, without fanfare, with little hope of success. They opened this obscure place on Harold Smith's twenty-fifth birthday. Hell, these upstarts, these carnival people, wouldn't last the winter. Nobody was a gaming success on Virginia Street. The hot action was over on Center Street, especially at the Bank Club. Dumb carnies. All they had was one beat-up old roulette wheel, lugged over the Sierra from their California carnival ventures, a wheel licensed by the City of Reno for $15 for three months.

Smith, the father, was born in 1887, the son of a poor beekeeper

in Addison Corners, Vermont; his father died when he was but six. Smith, who quit school at age fourteen, who in his eighty years had five wives, took fortune-tellers' words as the gospel and devoutly believed what the tea leaves said.

"Pappy" Smith was a promotional genius, the originator of Nevada ways of business life that today are commonplace.

They laughed at this carnie interloper through a few lean years. He had had the audacity to start a risky business in mid-Depression. By the late 1930s, his competitors, now grumbling, had taken sharp note.

From their fleabag operation underneath the old Charles Hotel, the Smiths grew, becoming millionaires many times over. Harolds Club exploded to become the biggest of the gaming biggies, propelled by "Pappy's" verve, nerve, creativeness. No plastic man. Plain, simple, sensitive to people.

"Pappy," remembering the "Pike's Peak or Bust" slogan from his days in Colorado, sprang the "Harolds Club or Bust" promotion on the country. He was the first gambler to go national and his 2,300 billboards, inviting folks to Harolds and to Reno, were a sensation. Done by young artist Lyle Ball of Reno, the signs cropped up in the Congo, in Casablanca, in the Antarctic—you name it, they were placed globally by the GIs of World War II.

"Pappy," folksy, holding his spiel down to a roaring yell, serving coffee and doughnuts to the boys on the troop trains parked a few feet away from Harolds Club's door; or prowling the club's interior, as he had done for thirty-two years, letting field mice gallop atop his gaming tables, the rodents darting into any of fifty holes that bettors hoped would be theirs; his unheard-of doubling of the players' bets; his glee when gamblers hit jumbo-size payoffs. "A winner is the best advertising in the world!"

For years, he forked over to heavy losers, enough money to get out of town; he was not the first to see the advantage of a four-lane Sierra superhighway to Reno, the fun town. But he certainly was the first to do something about getting it built. In concert with several people, especially Congressman Walter Baring, "Pappy" Smith finally got the four-lane Sierra route (Interstate 80) started.

"Pappy" was memorable because he, more than any other gambler, put his winnings back into his town and his state. This was the man who listened one day in 1946 to young Thomas C. Wilson, the advertising man. Smith had asked, "How can we return to Nevada the benefits we Smiths have received?" Answered Wilson, "Why not a scholarship to the University of Nevada-Reno, possibly $1,000 a year?" Bellowed "Pappy" to Wilson, "Why one? Let's give a $4,000 Harolds Club scholarship to a student from every high school, every year!" The scholarship was created and more than 250 high school graduates received, in aggregate, more than $1 million over the years, until the plan was scrapped because of adverse new tax laws.

"Pappy" donated the land where the Reno Elks Lodge now stands; he gave to churches, to historical research and on and on. He paid the medical bills and the burial bills of persons he hardly knew. He spent lavishly, seldom on himself.

He was the first to advertise "I lost my shirt," or "I lost my pants," an open confession of a known fact—that you don't ultimately win at gambling.

He played up fun because he loved fun, loved women, dancing, crowds, loved being unique, loved being a huge success.

He was a revolutionary man who managed change successfully and who initiated change.

Such a good, memorable man!

I wonder why they don't bring him flowers anymore.

NEVADA
PROFILES

He Wants to Quit Winners _____

NOBODY SLEEPS when Harold Smith, Sr., speaks. His raspy, booming voice belts out as if it was jammed through a high-volume public address system. As he sits with me during a long and pleasant interview, his quick hands jab the air, his way of punctuating his rapid, shouted sentences. Once an amateur boxer, he bobs and weaves in his chair. Now in his seventieth year, he is an old and scarred warrior. His health is frail, but his spirit is feisty. He is a man who earned millions, who has given away so much money he doesn't know how much, who has lost millions, and he is a man, if you please, who still wants to quit a winner.

Growing old isn't for sissies, and aging has been no picnic for the namesake of Harolds Club. Emphysema claws at him and is fueled by his four daily packs of unfiltered Camels. Arthritis has him in its painful grip, and aspirins help a little, damn little. Alcoholism has long been his nemesis, and he speaks frankly of it. "If you please, I have it whipped. I am on the wagon and I'm going to stay dry." He says his last drink was two and a half months ago.

But don't weep for Harold. He asked me to tell you he is a happy man. Listen:

Money: "I get a monthly Social Security check for $317. On top of that, I get two $900 checks a month from my attorney, who looks after my money. That's more than $2,000 a month, plenty to live on and still do a little gambling. Who could ask for anything more?"

Family: "The great reward of growing old is having grandchildren and I've got plenty—sixteen of 'em, and two of my granddaughters live with me. Julian Smith is a junior at Wooster High School, and Courtney Smith will be a freshman there next September. I drive those kids to school and back every day and I just love them. I just fell heir to them. Best thing that ever happened to me."

Education: "Tell the young people that I said to study. Study everything. Dig into the dictionary. Study Shakespeare, who wrote,

'Of all the wonders of this world, it seems most strange that man should fear the necessary end that will come when it will come.' At Harolds Club, we awarded more than 250 college scholarships, $4,000 each, to Nevada high school graduates. I don't know what happened to all those kids, but I betcha a lot of them prospered because of their schooling."

Gambling: "Don't gamble unless you know what you're doing. I'll gamble until I'm dead. Nobody is going to take it away from me. It's my life."

Wealth: "I spent plenty of money and I said it all with mink and diamonds and limousines. The money permitted me to bring the most famous stars in the world to Reno—Lily Pons, Jan Pearce, Isaac Stern and on and on. I had fun doing things that made people happy. I contend that to be happy, you have to make others happy."

Marriage: "Young people should get married and have kids and later have grandbabies. If you're old and alone, you get lonely. It shouldn't be that way."

Love: "I've been in love before, but now I'm really in love. I'm getting engaged and later I'm gonna marry. Her name is Eleanor Trulsen, who is sixty-two years old and lives in the San Francisco Bay area. Oh, how I love that woman!"

Honesty: "Hard work, coupled with honesty, can take you a long way. The young people of today, they should know it doesn't pay to cheat or to lie. Be honest with others and with yourself."

Friends: "Well, they really are worth more than gold. My truest friends have stuck by me. I'll always love them for not forgetting me. Nevadans are the greatest people anywhere, and I've been all over the world and I ought to know that there's no place as nice as your home."

My assets?: "Well, let me tell you young fella, there's been an ugly rumor around town for a long time that I am broke. That's poppycock. My attorney, Jack Streeter—I call him Hindu—he's got a 'spendthrift' clause on me. My net worth is more than a half-million, and I have plenty to live on each month, and to enjoy myself."

The media: "On balance, I've been treated well. When I was promoting my book *I Want to Quit Winners,* years ago, I was on all the TV talk shows. The newspapers? Well, a few years ago when I was at St. Mary's Hospital, the *Nevada State Journal* was very unkind to me. They interviewed me and took a picture with my hair all messed up. I haven't read the *Journal* since. It was a helluva thing to do to a guy who was sick."

Beauty: "One time, Richard Burton called me from Monterey and asked me to come over and visit. He was married to Elizabeth Taylor and, if you please sir, she was the most beautiful woman I've ever seen."

Religion: "I pray every day. I go to St. Thomas Aquinas Cathedral, and light candles for those I love. Sister Seraphine [of St. Mary's Hospital] is a saint, a tremendous person. St. Mary's has saved my life and I have done what I can to help the hospital."

Father: "My daddy [Raymond I. "Pappy" Smith] was a fantastic man. I remember him not just at Father's Day, but every day. Last week I went up to Harolds Club, where they have this bronze bust of him, and I put my hands on his face and I said, 'I love you, Daddy.'"

·§·§·§·§·

When Harold Smith, Sr., died in 1985 at the age of 75, he was eulogized as one of Nevada's greatest legalized-gaming pioneers.

Choosing a Campus Leader _____

I LIKE JOE.

Joe Crowley, interim president of the University of Nevada-Reno campus. Joe, the good guy. I like him because he is classy, witty and popular. I envy him the self-control that surfaces when he speaks privately and publicly.

I like Joe, as I do most guys who are white hat guys. I admit my bias for Joe is also caused by a certain knowledge that he is trustworthy, loyal, kind and won't let me put words in his mouth.

I would like Joe Crowley to be the next president of UNR. But I am not eligible to vote for Joe officially.

If five of the nine regents of the university system also like Joe enough to vote for him at a special meeting in Reno on Friday, then Joe will be the new UNR president.

Joe Crowley has earned regents' support because he is not a Joe Come Lately, not a babe in the Nevada political thicket; because he has the wisdom to be critical of himself, as well as of others; the instinct for remaining silent when appropriate, the sense to recognize what is realistic and what isn't; because within this low-key man is a reflective and firm man; his management style is participative, not autocratic; he is motivated toward a professional faculty; he is analytical and knows the danger of isolating himself from what's really happening outside his office.

I like Joe for UNR president because he has proven as the interim leader over thirteen months that he is indeed a leader, that he grasps new problems quickly and that he has the capacity to grow into a truly outstanding administrator.

Here is a man who refuses to rush into decisions before gathering facts, yet who knows the ultimate peril of administrative procrastination; he has pace, style and has refused at times to say yes, when it would have been expedient to agree.

I like Joe because he has courage, because he believes in students and understands why the ultimately best education cannot occur without sound leadership at the top.

He is the proper leader for this time and for the future.

He is the good guy and ablest leader, who should finish first.

The Nevada-Reno campus deserves no less.

·§·§·§·§·

One day after this column appeared, regents officially named Joe Crowley president of the University of Nevada-Reno. He passed his tenth anniversary in the position in February 1988.

Nevadan Fred Anderson _____

THE JUST-PUBLISHED oral history of eighty-year-old retired Reno physician Fred Anderson is fascinating and enlightening, laden with Nevada names and anecdotes and with behind-the-scenes glimpses of state higher education, medicine and politics.

Mary Ellen Glass, long before she retired as oral history program director at the University of Nevada-Reno, began in 1978 to record the urbane surgeon's recollections. But the death weeks later of his only son, Fred, Jr., also a physician, in a car accident so crushed Dr. Anderson that he lost the desire to finish the work. Fortunately for devotees of Nevada history, for scholars and even for this sophisticated man's critics, the history is now complete. The urgent cajoling, patience and diligent interviewing skill of Glass's successor, Thomas King, deserves sincere applause.

Dr. Anderson is now belittling his own oral document and I am among those who urge him to knock off the self-criticism. In fact, he rewards the reader with a candor that is the doctor's hallmark, pulling no punches, sparing neither Nevada doctors nor some of those with whom he served while a University of Nevada regent.

Frederick M. Anderson, born in 1906 in Elko County, showed no early hints he would be an overachiever. He was reared mostly in White Pine County by his bright, university-educated schoolteacher mother and his nonpracticing Mormon father, who had only an eighth-grade education, but who was a strong leader. The boy went to a one-room schoolhouse where half the pupils were Indian— there was the early taste of the underdog's plight. He was a teenager who once lost all his money playing poker with the grammar school principal, and who fell in love about every two years.

But while family talk keyed on farm prices, the weather and the condition of Anderson farm animals, he was devouring the Harvard classics, American history, wonderland books and *Encyclopaedia Britannica*. After high school (Ely) graduation, he worked a year at a pharmacy, dispensing ice cream sodas and patent medicine, saving up for college.

At the University of Nevada in Reno, he was scholar, bit-part actor, weekly *Sagebrush* editor, yearbook staff heavyweight. He even managed the Lambda Chi fraternity house in exchange for room and board.

In 1929, he was awarded the coveted Rhodes scholarship, one of only twenty-four Nevadans to win it from 1902 to 1986. Studying at great Oxford University in England on the Rhodes, he grew sophisticated, as well as smarter. From Oxford he went to another of the world's great learning places, Harvard University, to study medicine, his decision to be a doctor having been first triggered by the most influential man in his early life, UNR's legendary Peter (Bugs) Frandsen, biology department chairman and revered humanist.

The man with the rural roots practiced medicine for a half-century. He was the wartime doctor, treating trenchfoot from the Aleutian Islands, shiploads of malaria cases from South Pacific jungles, those with body wounds and those whose arms and legs had been blown away. As a civilian doctor in Carson City briefly, then in Reno, he was a general surgeon; he delivered babies; he looked after the pitiful children with polio lined up in iron lungs at Washoe Medical Center; he helped found Reno's poison control center; and he spent years helping drive cancer treatment quacks to retreat. He routinely worked fourteen-hour days, knowing he'd never be paid for charity cases, but feeling it was all worth it when he saved a life or felt the glow of new mothers ("They are the happiest patients").

He was for twenty-two years a university regent, with only Dr. Louis Lombardi (thirty years) and Silas Ross, Sr. (twenty-five), serving longer. He helped bring revolutionary changes in Nevada higher education—to name one—expansion to a statewide university system; he drove hard for gifts from the private sector; he led the establishment of the Nevada School of Medicine.

Dr. Anderson spent only $450 total in all his regent election efforts, such was the strength of his respected household name. He successfully urged no more than two consecutive regent chairperson terms ("The pain should be shared").

Behind Fred Anderson is quiet, classy Anne, who married him thirty-nine years ago. Public men's families too seldom get credit. Dr. Anderson has a telling comment about this: "I would have been a better doctor and father had I not spent so much time as a regent."

Lyle Ball—Nevada Artist _____

LYLE BALL looked across my desk during our interview and I saw a ruggedly handsome face, set under graying crew-cut hair. He is a solid six-foot-one, 200 pounds, appearing for all the world like an aging linebacker.

In fact, Lyle Ball has hardly been closer to football than the front of his TV set. He is an artistic institution in Reno; he is a man who probably has captured the real Nevada on canvas more times than any past or present painter.

In the past decade, after retiring from the Ball Sign Company that he founded a half-century ago, he has painted roughly 4,000 pictures.

Of course, one can be prolific and at the same time mediocre, or worse. What makes Lyle Ball exceptional is that he has been to his easel so often, yet maintained high levels of excellence.

He is being honored Tuesday at the annual Nevada Self Help Foundation recognition dinner at Bally Grand Hotel in Reno.

The speaker, Sue Wagner, state senator, will pay tribute to the man who was born in blizzard-snarled Reno on Christmas Eve, 1909.

He brightened, remembering the days growing up in Ball Canyon, west of Reno, a place named after his father's people. He was a young cowboy, the kid whose hands grew strong milking a string of cows, but who early on picked up chalk, went to the little blackboard in his home and began to draw. He would sketch all manner of things then.

When he became a young adult, he turned to art to make a living. He was drawing grocery display signs fresh out of high school, then arranging window displays for businesses.

Ultimately, he started up the one-man Ball Sign Company. His first studio was his bedroom.

Earlier, he had the good fortune to marry Esther Flanary, the daughter of a Sparks railroader. He laughs, "I like to joke that I found my wife at Sears, Roebuck—we both worked there when we first met."

The seventy-seven-year-old Nevadan gravitated naturally to the art medium he is most comfortable with and adept at—watercolors—because with Ball Sign Company he did speculation art for neon signs in watercolors and painted watercolor renderings of proposed new structures for Reno architects.

He did perhaps twenty-five watercolor paintings a year before his retirement from Ball Sign, then went to his easel full-time ten years ago.

His signature is a familiar one among buyers and his trademark subject is invariably Nevada—vivid colors, applied with bold strokes, take his viewers to venerable Eureka County buildings, the sagging old Verdi barns, the majestic old Fourth Ward Schoolhouse on the Comstock and Reno's long-gone grammar schools.

Lyle Ball's work shows Nevada's towering peaks and lovely valleys, with their spectacular array of colors; here, a scene along the Nevada-Utah border; there, the ghost towns. The man prowling Belmont and Wonder and the Reese River always lugs along his camera.

His work is the sagebrush, the yawning spaces, the snow-fed Truckee, our rock-strewn desert landscape. "I think," he states, "that if anyone remembers me, it will be for my love of our state, for its old mining towns, its lovely old ranch homes and our incomparable skies, meadowlands and the trees. God, how I love trees." Ball never wanted to be a portrait painter, but he learned early to draw men and livestock.

He considers himself lucky to have watched so much history occur in his town, and he likes to talk about the characters he's known.

Raymond I. "Pappy" Smith was the most creative man he ever met. It was Ball who first drew the "Harolds Club or Bust" promotions that were to ignite national attention for Harolds.

George Wingfield, Sr., "a pudgy little guy and a strong-willed person, used to call me 'boy,'" he recalls.

Of the outstanding Nevada artists, now gone, he remembers foremost J. Craig Sheppard ("a wonderful man who should have lived longer"), Robert Caples ("delicate, refined, tremendously talented") and Hans Meyer-Kassel ("our best artistic transplant ever").

Lyle Ball is about to get back on top of his art form after being hospitalized with a bleeding ulcer. He is excited about his dinner. But no more excited than those who'll be there to wish him well and to thank this remarkable man for his contributions.

The Abortion Fighter _____

MINUTES PRIOR to today's 12:30 Mass at St. Thomas Aquinas Cathedral, near downtown Reno, Charles "Andy" Anderson will drive up in his tired Pinto station wagon, the one with more than 106,000 miles on it, the same blue Ford jalopy with the amateurishly drawn antiabortion slogans affixed to it. He'll park as close to the Catholic church as he can get. Thank the Lord he won't have to feed the meter, because this is Sunday. Anderson then will help his invalid wife into the wheelchair. Inside, the clergy will talk about history.

Anderson and Christians around the world know the Palm Sunday story by heart. On the first Palm Sunday, twenty centuries ago, the Man rode His donkey into town over a pathway strewn with palms. It was the people's way of glorifying Him, for they adored Him. But a lot of politicians were out to get Him and, as it turned out, too many of His supporters were fair-weather friends. Just thirty-three was this most controversial Man, and five days later the enemies murdered Him. But on Easter Sunday, there occurred the Miracle of the Ages. He rose from the dead. He has since become the most influential person of the last two thousand years.

"Andy" Anderson, friend of Jesus Christ, is never going to be famous. The span of Anderson's influence may be a little wider than a few peanuts, the crop that grows down around Savannah, Georgia, near where Anderson was born and reared.

Except for his wife Marie, who had a stroke in 1975, I haven't found anyone who adores "Andy" Anderson. To be sure, a few persons gawk with surprise and perhaps even faint admiration at his antiabortion campaign. But to the majority who see him picket, or who observe his weary Ford, laden with a toy infant in a cradle and those "Abortion is a deadly evil" signs—well, can you blame them for wondering, "What is this guy, some kind of nut?"

Friends, if you ever believed anything I've written for your eyes, believe this: Charles "Andy" Anderson is most definitely not crazy. A glutton for punishment, yes. But crazy? No way!

Anderson is a most gentle man, but his pugilist features look like Joe Louis hit him first, and then Marciano and Ali added a few licks for additional measure. A retired career air force noncommissioned officer, he was an amateur boxer whose face was fodder for more skilled military fighters.

Anderson is graying, articulate, intelligent and he wears an old felt hat ($2, St. Vincent's Thrift Shop) and clean but tired old clothes (more bargains from the thrift shop). Under the worse-for-wear garments is a freshly scrubbed Anderson, fingernails meticulously clean; Anderson, the one-man orator, so convincing he could peddle a Frigidaire in a North Pole ice factory. But Anderson, skimping along on his $350 air force retirement pay, isn't selling anything but antiabortion.

His solo campaign is in its fifth year. In 1975 a young Nevada woman friend, whom he does not identify, went to an abortion clinic in Oakland. She called him in Reno. Anderson went to his knees and he begged his friend not to go through with it. She paid him no heed. She died.

Anderson has depleted his life savings to combat what he terms the "slaying of the defenseless unborn." What has been the material price? After Marie Anderson's disabling massive stroke, they sold their three-bedroom home off old Geiger Grade Road, got $20,000 net, used $15,000 to pay her medical and hospital bills and spent the balance on his antiabortion campaign. They live in a clean, cluttered apartment a few blocks from St. Mary's Hospital.

Publicly, Anderson is about as popular as the chieftain at the world's most contagious leper colony. He was invited to his last dinner at any close friend's house years ago. To the Abortion Assortment, he is the enemy—committed, tireless, weird.

There is one chief difference between the Vietnam protesters of the late 1960s and early 1970s and "Andy" Anderson. They numbered in the millions. He is alone.

What price? His old car has been tormented by vandals. Hate messages are scrawled in lipstick on the windshield. He has been spit on, shoved, cussed, hit. He was arrested by Reno police on September 18, 1979, after he picketed a proabortion meeting at the Pioneer Inn. Charged with offensive conduct, he was fingerprinted and jailed for three hours. As he left the police station on his own recognizance, a policeman smiled: "Now, I suppose you're gonna go over to the Truckee River and walk on water!" Anderson smiled back and offered his stock reply to critics: "God loves you. So do I. While I might tread water for a while, I've only heard of one Man who could walk on it."

Ugly notes pile up around his car. "You are sick!" "You narrow-minded exhibitionist." "An abortion a day keeps the baby away." The man campaigns on. Shorn of his savings, he feels he is a rich man. One person wrote Anderson not long ago: "His Holiness wishes you to know he will pray for your special intention." The note was signed by Pope John Paul II.

Portrait of a Photographer _____

A FEISTY TEENAGER, Marilyn Newton, waltzed into our newsroom as a fresh hire twenty years ago this month. She was eighteen, bouncy, full of verve, swerve and nerve. She had the guts of a burglar.

She was a fresh punk of a kid, so we stuck her in a corner in a clerical job, hoping she'd learn something, such as respect for her newspaper elders. I was a young editor at the time, but considerably older than Newton, and in my so-called journalism wisdom of 1963, I didn't give her a plug-nickel of a chance to stay on the payroll. Too sassy and grassy green and undisciplined, thought I. Which goes to show you my judgment was flawed then, too.

Within her first week, Marilyn Newton busted away from her little blizzard of clerical paperwork long enough to write a page-one by-line story about the first installation of a pacemaker at a Reno hospital.

In less than six months, she convinced the young management of the *Reno Evening Gazette* that she knew which end of a camera to load the film in. Thus, she began two decades of photographing the shiniest, grimiest news events in this part of Nevada.

Every newspaper reader here has seen her pictures and credit lines. Or watched her at news events—athletic contests, accident scenes and other maimings.

Newton is the filly who stalks the law enforcement scene like Elmer's Glue. Few things in the world of crime and gore escape her. Her police radio is blaring constantly; she sleeps with a direct line into the cop shops and her lawman sources are here, there, everywhere.

The *Gazette-Journal*'s former executive editor Bob Ritter said, "I've never seen a photographer so consistently able to get quality hard news shots. Marilyn has the instincts, the sources and the willingness to roll hard twenty-four hours a day."

Roll hard is a precise way of defining our Marilyn Newton. To drive with her at the wheel, to an accident scene, a fire or other catastrophe, is to experience sheer terror.

She is the photographer who once drove wildly across Reno in pursuit of a man who'd just killed his wife. She caught up with the guy at the police roadblock and shot prize-winning pictures.

She's fallen down stairs, been tackled at football games and been bucked off camels—all for the love of capturing the story on film.

One dark night on Geiger Grade in 1971, she was shot at while scrambling down a hill to photograph a fatal accident. She wasn't hurt and luckily for the sniper she never got her hands on him. She's got a lot of wildcat in her when aroused.

She's been a first-place prizewinner seven straight years in the National Press Women's competition—once for a news story and the other times for her photographs.

Her gravitation to the law enforcement scene is natural. Her father, Charles, was a career officer in Carson City and her identical twin, Elaine Newton, who died in 1982, was a Washoe County Sheriff's deputy. And some of the people she most respects have been from the law scene, among them the late Reno assistant police chief William Brodhead, "one of the outstanding men ever," and former sheriff Bob Galli, "a tough, humane cop who was respected by his men."

But to suggest that Marilyn follows the crime-accident-fire scene exclusively is to give you a false impression. She's the one who also brings gentle pictures of children and adults at play; she's among our people who capture Sam Mosley's basketball slam dunks and rodeo action; and she's the one who in 1964 plopped herself on the fender of Lyndon Johnson's black limousine and who wouldn't budge until the Secret Service let her get exclusive pictures of the president.

In private life, she's single—"I married three times and struck out each time. I guess you might say I'm a slow learner."

Her hobbies: on her days off, she's often in the Nevada desert, photographing wildlife and other marvels of that scenery, or prowling antique shops in quest of bargains, or off dining on morsels that help keep 115 pounds on her five-foot-two frame—things like steak, potatoes and chocolate cake.

What she loves so much about her newspaper work is that it brings her close to life and makes her appreciate how truly precious it is. She has photographed all aspects of life—from the happiest to the most tragic events—and these experiences reinforce her belief that every life and every death has a purpose.

As to how she differs from that eighteen-year-old filly first encountered twenty years ago this month, well, now she's thirty-eight, but nothing much else has changed.

Blue-eyed Marilyn, the girl with the big smile, remains sassy, feisty, bouncy, full of verve, swerve and nerve. And ready for the next assignment in her favorite world—people making news.

Ben Dasher

LAST TUESDAY was Ben Dasher's sixty-fifth birthday and it also was his final day as chief executive officer of Universe Life Insurance Company, a firm he founded thirty-five years ago in Reno. Then, he had a pencil, a tiny office, one employee besides himself and plenty of hope.

Today, this remarkable man of integrity, intellect, patience and commanding presence leaves Universe, which is numbered among the country's most respected and most successful insurance firms, to the care of others. He has reached the mandatory retirement age.

Two special events marked Dasher's retirement. At a Prospectors Club reception, he cracked, with a sly wink at wife Helen: "After retirement, a wife gets twice as much husband and half as much pay."

At a luncheon with his Universe insurance colleagues, he was typical Dasher: "My eye is not dim and my arrow is still finding its mark, and you're going to continue seeing me around."

This part of Nevada wouldn't be the same without Ben Dasher, whose zest, leadership and continuing hope are unexcelled. Dasher would dispute that, but the men and women who've worked with him in business and on civic projects would, I am certain, vote him civic leader of every year. His superb organizational style, his ability to delegate and his superior skill of shaping people into harmonious teams have caused business and public sectors to scramble for his leadership.

He has been a productive follower and/or leader in youth work, banking, and United Way as well as for the School of Medicine of the University of Nevada System, hospitals, Sierra Pacific Power Company (director), the Chamber of Commerce (president, two terms), the Home Savings and Loan Association, and athletics; and he will continue as leader of the Harrah Automobile Foundation.

Dasher has established his own Reno insurance consulting firm, to which he will bring great experience, and a philosophy that glows. As a physical presence, he will continue to be impossible to ignore. Dasher is six-foot-five, a fellow who as a teenager shoveled coal on Lake Erie ore boats eight hours a day and grew to 240 pounds of muscle. He looks like he could still shovel with the strongest of them.

He has a smile that would warm an igloo.

His philosophy emerged in an interview he and I had Wednesday.

Success path: "Go full-heartedly into your work. Give a full dollar's worth to your employer. Don't cogitate too much about what you get back, for that takes care of itself. I'm not a great believer in job-jumping because most of the time the promised land is where you are now."

Company success: "I've never seen a successful company yet that didn't have top people."

Adversity: "At least fifty percent of any competitive endeavor is frustration. The trick is not to permit adversity to produce overriding discouragement. It has been my experience that something almost always comes along, sometimes unexpectedly, that results in victory."

Eureka!: "Once in a while you read about the person who finds a gold nugget (scores a dazzling victory in one fell swoop). But it's not your everyday occurrence."

Pacing to goals: "I've never been a believer—in business or in any other endeavor—in the so-called long touchdown run. My experience is that reaching goals is a grind no matter what you're doing. Move ahead a mile, get set back three-quarters of a mile."

Patience: "Once you find the business that will make the best use of your talents, stay there and concentrate. All of us have seen valuable talent go down the drain because "they" thought the grass was greener on the other side."

Time's passage: "The years have passed fast, yes, but not in the sense that I wonder where they went. I know where they went. I don't regret being sixty-five. I love it, just as I've loved every prior time."

Wounds: "We all experience hurt along the way. But the mind is a great healer, gently wrapping scar tissue around the negatives and making us well again."

Marriage: "A person in business today has enough frustrations without additional problems at home. Problems are cut in half when you have a supportive spouse. And that, I have." (Helen and Ben Dasher are in their thirty-fifth year as wife and husband.)

Freedom: "It is so wonderful, but let us remember that freedom also carries with it the responsibility not to misuse or take for granted that freedom."

Nevada: "To an outsider, we at first appear to be a forbidding state. I laugh at that attitude. Our state is the greatest."

Agent Burau of the FBI _____

YOUR NAME is Douglas Lowell Burau, age fifty-one, a resident of southwest Reno since 1967. You are a husband, father, American and for twenty-six years, despite your peace-loving nature, you packed a loaded, snub-nosed revolver to work every day. You are descended from the American poet, James Russell Lowell, and the kind of personal poetry you most revere and live by goes like this: "My country 'tis of thee, sweet land of liberty."

In your first career, you were regarded as a great professional. Yet, today is the first time your story and photograph ever have been published in a newspaper. That's because you've been, since 1953, Doug Burau of the FBI. The job of all the 8,500 agents has been to protect the United States from outside and inside menace. In other words, get the bad guys off the streets and into the slammers where they belong. To do that, you've had to travel incognito, fighting stealth with stealth, using anonymity to its maximum advantage.

But five days ago, you became Burau, formerly of the FBI. Now your story can be told, for you have retired after a distinguished career.

You are Doug Burau (pronounced like bureau), and in the history of the Federal Bureau of Investigation dating to 1908, you are the only agent with that last name—and it's been a source of confusion and amusement. "I'm Burau from the Bureau."

A native of North Dakota, you grew up in Grand Forks. You and all the boys in your graduating high school class enlisted in the navy en masse near the end of World War II. After the war, you worked your way through college as a trumpet player in Midwest bands. And then it was on to law school and by now you were married, the father of a son, working part-time in a clothing store, also earning $15 a night blowing the horn and going to law school by day. And you were graduated in the top ten, managing somehow to pay the rent on your little apartment and to stake the family to enough grub.

Finally, came your longtime dream: to be with the FBI. To become an agent in those days, you had to be either a lawyer or an accountant with three years of experience.

You passed the FBI's tough standards easily and became an agent in 1953, taking training in Washington and at Quantico, Virginia.

You look back on those twenty-six years at so many things you did as an FBI team player. Years ago, the FBI's concentration was on car thieves, military deserters, draft dodgers, bank robbers and counterintelligence. Times change for all of us, including the criminals. Today, the crime ball park is crowded with sophisticated swindlers, dope pushers, airplane hijackers, computer manipulators, kidnappers and, as always, bank holdup men.

Your years of service were packed with painstaking detail work, with danger, with the sweet thrill of success and with frustration when the pursued got away. There were your rookie days in the Kansas City FBI bureau, and the first big case you worked on: the kidnapping of little Bobby Greenlease—you and other agents, trying to plant hundreds of thousands in marked bills with suspects and then the tragic conclusion: finding the body of the murdered boy.

Then on to New York City in the days when the Red Scare and Senator Joe McCarthy were the No. 1 story in the nation. And you, Doug Burau, tailing known and suspected Communists; or you, Burau, a white man, working as a lone agent in Harlem.

The most memorable day of your life occurred in 1967 when you were admitted to practice before the U.S. Supreme Court and that very day met for the first and only time the most famous crime fighter of all, J. Edgar Hoover. The FBI chief, an awesome figure, inquired about your family and told you that enemies within wanted to see the destruction of the FBI, but that it would outlive its critics. They took your photograph with the chief, and you've got it on the wall of your home.

And thence to Reno twelve years ago. Here, you've always been the team man, tenacious, imaginative, thinking as the fugitive thinks: "I've committed a crime. I'm on the run. What will I do?" You, Burau, running up the national colors every morning in your front yard, and then running down the enemy by day, or however long it requires. Never a day that was the same: working extortions, hijackings and many hostage situations, including five involving Reno area banks.

145

You've remained all these years Doug Burau, a man so conservative that colleagues claim you are to the right of Attila the Hun, and that you make Ronald Reagan look like a liberal. Burau, the master of semantics, whose cool soft sell coaxed many a confession and surrender. Burau, known by fellow agents as the great humor man who nicknamed his colleagues such things as "The Verdi Monk," "The Grinch," "The Silver Fox" and "The Bathroom Repairman."

They'll remember you also as Doug Burau, whose knowledge of the law has helped make convictions a certainty. In this era of changing Supreme Court stances, some of them favoring the criminal (columnist's firm bias), your legal expertise has helped keep the baddies locked up.

You'll never forget, Doug Burau, when you and wife Edna told your little daughter Jody that "Daddy is retiring," and how the girl wept, saying, "But Daddy, I'm the only one at my school who has a father who's with the FBI!"

You've got a second career now. You'll become manager of the State Contractors Board, and you'll remain in Reno. As for local law enforcement, you know it's in great hands, because you've worked part and parcel with the Reno and Sparks police, the sheriff's people and the State Highway Patrol.

Burau family involvement in law enforcement carries on. There is your oldest son Steve, a Secret Service man guarding Vice-President Walter Mondale, and second son Scott, a Carson City sheriff's deputy.

They gave you a farewell retirement party last week. You and Edna were front and center and you got the memento gifts and you, the tough and fair FBI man who never lost his cool, said, "A man once said you are rich if you have a good wife, good kids, good health and good friends. So I guess I gotta be the richest guy in the world." You choked up at the end, Doug Burau, as everyone stood and applauded you. It was their way of saying happy voyage and thank you.

A Visit with Governor Russell _____

TODAY IS THE seventy-fifth birthday of Charles H. Russell, the two-term Nevada governor of the 1950s. He and his wife Marjorie are observing the event quietly and happily in Carson City.

Happily, because for the first time in eight years, all of the five Russell children are with their parents during the holiday season.

Quietly, because Governor Russell can no longer endure long observances.

The family will wind down father's seventh-fifth tonight, rallying for dinner at the Ormsby House, giving him gifts and affection. Governor Russell will accept everything quietly—his way—but he'll be mighty pleased, as always.

Governor Russell was never a flashy chief executive. He wasn't the silver-tongued orator. He campaigned for public office on anemic budgets and relied on personal contact and radio to hustle support. His public career occurred before television was a big campaigning deal.

What a career! The Lovelock native was: Nevada assemblyman; state senator; one-term congressman; two-term governor; U.S. diplomat to Paraguay. Finally, he was a University of Nevada fundraiser for four years.

He and Marjorie and the children left the Governor's Mansion twenty years ago this month, when he was fifty-five. His eight gubernatorial years were jammed with accomplishments. Charles Russell did everything so quietly you hardly knew he was assembling a great base from which future governors could operate. He made all his successors look good. Among other things, here is what Governor Russell contributed:

—Established the state's first genuine gaming control agency, making control a professional activity and thus thwarting organized crime, which thirsted then for pieces of the action.

—Overhauled the state school system, knocking out the unmanageable 230-odd school districts and reducing the system to 17 districts.

—Initiated steps that led to the establishment of the state's Department of Conservation and Natural Resources, which became an umbrella for various environmental agencies.

—Dealt effectively with the postwar baby boom, calling a special legislative session to solve the problems of school overcrowding and inadequate financing and organization in education.

—With his evenhandedness kept the controversial Nevada higher education turmoil from worsening.

He had guts. In 1957, certain gaming interests used their Senate Bill 92 in an effort to suspend gaming regulations that Russell had been instrumental in making into law. Russell was faced with substantial public opposition and gaming's powerful behind-the-scenes maneuvering. He vetoed the bill and was upheld by one vote.

Earlier, when he was in Congress, he had voted for the Taft-Hartley bill. Nevada senators Patrick McCarran and George Malone had voted against it.

Russell paid dearly. Organized labor made certain he lost his re-election bid to Walter Baring.

He did not make a nest egg in public life. The first years he was governor, he was paid $7,600 a year. In his first two years as chief executive, he drove his own car to work, getting only mileage pay. It was only in his brief tenure as a diplomat that he and Marjorie were able to squirrel away some savings.

As governor, he was absolutely honest and he had courage underneath that shy reserve.

When I visited the Russells in their modest three-bedroom Carson City home, he recalled the past. Mrs. Russell would help occasionally. He took me on a house tour, pointed proudly at political mementos, but especially at the antiques the couple has collected over the years.

Daughter Virginia Sakal, of Hamilton, New York, put some fruitcake in front of us. But her blue eyes twinkled. "Father, you can't have any of this."

Mrs. Russell said, "Charles, be sure and tell how I loaned you $2,000 to run for Congress."

Grandchildren marched in and out during the visit. "Grandpa, may I have a cookie?" "Grandpa, when is lunch?"

Governor and Mrs. Russell live quietly these days. He shuns TV like the black plague, preferring to read mystery stories. Together, the couple chases down antiques to add to the collection.

Both love to reflect on when they met.

An aunt suggested in 1938, "Charlie, there's a girl you must meet—Marjorie Guild." The aunt arranged a dinner. He was captivated by the pretty, brown-eyed Ruth, Nevada, schoolteacher, who was a Carson City native.

The following March, she became Mrs. Charles H. Russell. Wife of—if you'll pardon the cliché—one of the nicest and ablest men who ever came down the Nevada pike.

IN MEMORIAM

Against Great Odds _____

BY ORDINARY ODDS, Edward A. Olsen should have died of a terrible affliction when he was yet an infant. If not that, he should have endured a hopeless invalid's life, unable to care for himself or to contribute to society. Absent that fate, he should have died of 1954 car accident injuries that mangled a body already singled out for special physical torment. Instead, Ed Olsen successfully defied a succession of overwhelming adversities. Until the final adversity.

He died this week of emphysema at the age of fifty-nine. The illness was the final unfair stroke dealt to an absolutely fair man.

In his life as a Nevadan—which was most of his adult life—Olsen was first an extraordinarily gifted and productive newsman; then a most outstanding Nevada Gaming Control Board chairman; then for ten years, until illness cut him down, he was the effective and trustworthy public relations voice of the University of Nevada.

Ed Olsen was no ordinary man, as the thousands who knew and respected him are quite aware. But few of that legion of admirers knew of his difficult childhood, until after his death. It was painful for Ed to recall his childhood, but he did speak of those years a decade ago, giving his own history to Mary Ellen Glass of UNR's Oral History Project. Ed had stipulated that his history not be available to the public until after his death.

He was born in Brooklyn in 1919, the son of a second-generation Norwegian father and a teenage Irish mother. Agnes Murtha Olsen was tubercular and TB infected her baby, causing the loss of hip joints. The parents moved to Denver when he was an infant.

His first eleven years were spent in hospitals, in body-casts and in surgery, with chloroform as the anesthetic. A tutor visited the children's bedsides. Though handicapped physically, Ed Olsen was a star pupil from the start. He learned to type, flat on his back, sweltering in a full-length cast.

Ed, when he was in the early teens, matriculated from casts to a wheelchair, then to crutches and finally to a cane. He remembered a teacher in high school looking at him and then telling others in the class, "Don't call a cripple a cripple."

He got through the high school years, his intellect apparent to all. Then, with his father and supportive stepmother (his own mother died when Ed was three or four) urging him on, he enrolled at the University of Colorado, majoring in journalism.

He met his future wife on campus. Dorothy Douglass was the daughter of Colorado's dean of education and she was a journalism major, too. After Ed's junior year, the couple married. It was still the Depression and jobs were scarce for journeymen, let alone for two kids in love. But they worked up a joint résumé, labeling it "Two for the Price of One."

Then on to Oregon, with Ed working for a succession of under-financed, struggling publications.

In the early World War II years, the Olsens moved to Boise, Idaho, where Olsen took on multiple duties with the *Idaho States-man*. He grew fast on all jobs, a top young bright guy with lame legs and a great mind.

Olsen joined the Associated Press wire service in 1944, in the Boise bureau, taking a cut in pay. In little over a year, an AP opening came in the Reno bureau, and Olsen got the job, despite his youth. The year was 1945.

He held the job for Reno AP for fifteen years, covering the great, the near-great, the infamous. Olsen was one of the first to de-tect Senator Joseph McCarthy, the red-hunter, for what he was, a phony. "Nevada Senator Pat McCarran was Mr. God." Actress Rita Hayworth, in Nevada for a divorce, was a very special, thoughtful woman. There was an endless parade of big stories, in which Ed Olsen usually seemed a step ahead of competitors—floods; the big divorce parade of those years; the trapped City of San Francisco train atop Donner Summit; the burglary from the Reno home of LaVere Redfield of millions; and countless other stories that are part of our history.

Adversity came down hard again in 1954. Dorothy and Ed had built themselves a little home west of Reno, off old Highway 40. There was the terrible head-on crash, with the other driver at fault. Dorothy dead. Ed near-dead, carted to a place he knew so well as a child—the hospital. Months of pain, of repair by great Reno sur-geons—again, Ed Olsen's fighting spirit brought him home alive.

Finally, in 1955, he was back in the AP bureau in Reno—the top pro, walking again, the cheater of long odds.

The Associated Press had been after Ed Olsen to take other bigger assignments. Finally, in 1959, he reluctantly agreed to take the AP job in Sacramento. He lasted a year, winning plaudits of the wire service and his California colleagues, but missing his home, Nevada, every minute. Finally, he resigned.

He came home in 1960. Governor Grant Sawyer's goals included getting the best man he knew to head up the vital Gaming Control Board. Olsen became chairman, holding that job through Sawyer's two terms. It was early in the decade when Olsen showed that he was not only brilliant, but tough as well. His knock-down, drag-out fight with entertainer Frank Sinatra has been told often this past week and before, and I'll not dwell on it here, save to say that Sinatra, with all his influence, could not make Olsen back down from the law and principle. Sinatra gave up his attempt to retain casino ownership at Lake Tahoe. Olsen was a winner again.

When Sawyer left office, Olsen left the gaming job. He was dynamite in his decade as UNR news chief. Everyone trusted him, believed in him.

In his own productive and great life, Ed Olsen did it his way. Superior in all he attempted and did. A man who found joy in doing things well, and in doing things for others. He was a great teacher who taught by example.

The best example was his own life. He refused to be handicapped. He decided to be great instead.

The Story of Mia _____

MIRANDA "Mia" Hulme was beautiful evidence that talent isn't wasted on the young. Though barely thirty, she had already established herself in Reno business as an enterprising and creative leader and as one who wreathed herself in courtesy and grace.

Ask anyone who knew her, friends or family, and the analysis is the same: "Mia has everything going for her."

"Mia was one of the finest employees I ever had," recalls furrier Les Conklin. "And I never met a nicer person." To her former Conklin's co-worker Laura Kerin, "She was the epitome of class." Her stepmother put it in another way. "Mia," said Doramae Jakobson, "could walk into a room on an overcast day and light it up. She was sunshine."

Born in The Hague, Netherlands, she was barely five feet tall and had to struggle to keep up to 100 pounds. She was of fair complexion and had blonde hair and blue eyes—Scandinavian good looks. It was her professional record and her potential that excited admirers most. You could define her future as you would her past with a word: promise.

When she was in only her early twenties, Conklin signed her and sent her to San Francisco to train in the art of repair, cleaning and storage of furs. She became an excellent technician. Mia's early schooling in fashion design in Stockholm, Sweden, reinforced her success with Conklin in the late 1970s and early 1980s.

It was after she married Tom Hulme on Valentine's Day, four and a half years ago, that she turned professional commitment from working for others to founding her own enterprise. "I hated to lose her," said Conklin, "but when she told me she wished to strike out on her own, I had to applaud her zeal and her striking good promise."

Her start-up was modest. She first opened the little alterations shop over on Hillcrest. As she confirmed her worth as a dress designer and tailor to Greater Reno clientele, projects poured in. She outgrew the shop. Next stop? Miranda's Ladies' Tailoring, her attractive and efficiently managed business in Moana West Shopping Center.

Volume grew brisk. In only a few months, her enterprise brewing smoothly, she had four women on the Hulme payroll. The patrons and the matrons liked her expertise and her personal warmth. Tailoring is an art form. She was an artist.

A happy marriage was her life's frosting.

Mia's father, Incline realtor Bert Jakobson, had given the couple a small condo as a wedding gift. Now, with Tom's good job as manager of a cheese shop at Greenbrae and her own business success, they traded up, acquiring a bigger home, in Sky Ranch Estates, off the Pyramid Lake Highway six miles north of Sparks.

They called it their dream home. How they were working to make it even dreamier! Each was putting in twelve to fourteen hours a day at work. They were dolling up the three-bedroom home and the next project was to fence their acre so the two dogs could roam free.

Thirteen nights ago, each worked late, she on a personal project: creating and making stepmother Doramae's satin dress, to be worn to the fortieth reunion of Reno High School's class of 1943.

Tom and Mia, driving in their own cars, met after work for the dinner that would be their last together.

Then she drove away first from the restaurant on South Virginia Street and Tom was close behind.

It was shortly after 10 o'clock that night and she was alone on dark Pyramid Road. If Mia glanced in the rearview mirror to spot Tom, she couldn't, for he had been slowed by traffic and was three minutes behind.

A car approached from the opposite direction. In the final moments of Mia's life, she saw the headlights come across the center line straight at her. There was no time to steer from the peril that rushed at her too swiftly.

Minutes later, Tom Hulme came upon the accident. He saw that it was Mia's car. He was there in shock, in disbelief and in grief as authorities removed Mia's body.

The other driver, a Reno man, was taken to the hospital and treated for minor scrapes. Blood tests were taken. They showed he had consumed twice the amount of alcohol required to deem one legally drunk. The police booked him for felony DUI. This is the third time he has faced a DUI charge. Twice before his penalty was a light fine and suspended jail term.

At Mia's memorial service, Les Conklin went to embrace Mia's father. He saw the ultimate sorrow in the face of the man who lost his only child.

A Prayer for Clare ⸻

ON THE FACE OF IT, Clare Parre's global qualities didn't square with her background. She was reared in Kansas, came west as a young woman, moved to Reno and never traveled beyond her country's borders.

She never studied foreign languages and her little Cherokee, Kansas, home wasn't exactly a bubbling ethnic pot. Yet, for going on two decades on the University of Nevada-Reno campus, she became a sort of "mother to all races." At UNR, Mrs. Parre lighted every sector of campus with an endearing personality and a candid streak that earned her respect. It was her closeness with foreign students that was her most enduring achievement.

When she died last week after a long illness with cancer, there was grieving that brought the campus closer together for she had a universal appeal, a way of unifying people regardless of the language they spoke or the name of the Holy Author they worshiped or the color of their skin.

At a memorial service, friends testified to her goodness and colleague K. B. Rao, who came to Reno and UNR eight years ago by way of New York and his native India, told a story.

Two years ago, Dr. Rao had to go to Fallon to speak to a group about reincarnation. He does not drive, so he asked Clare Parre to take him. During the Fallon speech, he gave a special prayer.

Later, as they drove through the darkness back to Reno, Mrs. Parre, her cancer then in remission, said to him, "K. B., if anything happens to me, use that quotation at my service."

At her memorial service, he again spoke the prayer:

> Do not stand at my grave and weep:
> I am not there. I do not sleep.
> I am a thousand winds that blow.
> I am the diamond glints on snow.
> I am the sunlight of ripened grain.

I am the gentle autumn rain.
When you awaken in the morning's hush,
I am the swift uplifting rush
Of quiet birds in circled flight,
I am the soft stars that shine at night.
Do not stand at my grave and cry;
I am not there; I did not die.*

---

*Poem from *A Sense of Honor* by James Webb (Englewood Cliffs, N.J.: Prentice-Hall, 1981).

Editor Paul Leonard _____

FOR SIX NIGHTS a week, through the sixteen years he was editor of the *Nevada State Journal*, Paul Leonard did his best work while most Nevadans slept. The years were 1957 to 1972; the *Journal* was a morning newspaper, as it is today, and Leonard usually reached his office in the early afternoon.

He would attend to the myriad of editor's duties into the late evening. They put the paper to bed—"Good morning, Mr. and Mrs. Nevada, let's go to press"—close to midnight. Then everyone except Paul Leonard went home. He remained to write viewpoints.

In my mind's eye, I see him yet today, alone with his thoughts, his angular frame leaning into his typewriter. First peering at blank paper, then pecking away in the methodical way he had of attacking his writing chore. Sometimes he completely rewrote, but most often he heavily edited his opinion pieces with the ever-present copy pencil. He usually made it home by 4 A.M.

He made millions of words appear out of thin air on a multitude of topics. He was the chief news executive of a paper that purported to be liberal. But Paul Leonard was alternately middle-of-the-road or to the left or, on another night, conservative.

He was at all times as honest as he could be. None of the thousands of subjects he tackled was exactly like another. Thus, he could not make them the same.

Leonard died a month short of his seventy-sixth birthday. The obituary noted he had written an estimated 6,000 editorials, a statistic that came from Paul Leonard himself, in an interview given not long after his 1972 retirement. As usual, he understated, by a wide margin, his own skill. In fact, the *Journal* converted from a six-day-a-week publication to seven mornings, not long after the Fallon native was installed as editor.

For the next decade and a half, he averaged two editorials a day, invariably on Nevada topics. A total of 15,000 opinion pieces is a more reasonable estimate of his production.

It wasn't the high numbers that mattered, but the breadth of his subjects and, above all, his reasonableness. Paul Leonard had rural roots, had lived out in Ely and Elko, had been to college and to war, had experienced bigger city living. He had acquired much wisdom during his upbringing, knowledge that a covey of role models reinforced, among them, University of Nevada journalism professor A. L. Higginbotham and *Elko Daily Free Press* editor Chris Sheerin.

Leonard informed himself thoroughly on his subjects. He was a creative listener whose interviewing style was engaging because he himself was a warm and trustworthy man. His opinions were reasoned and he invariably laid a strong foundation at the outset of an editorial, before offering a final opinion. He was the man a state trusted, the person his city turned to for leadership. For sixteen years, he gave his best.

He was a delightful, happy man whose pixie wit came out in print and in person; he laughed at himself and, if there was a kinder man, I never met him.

Newspaper organizations, like other companies, are quite human. Internal politics visit us, too. Paul Leonard avoided getting snared in such maneuvering. At one period, I was an editor competing with him. Later, I was *Gazette-Journal* publisher—Paul Leonard's boss. I knew him, as others knew him, as a man without guile who had the irresistible credential called goodness. When you dealt with Paul Leonard, you felt safe.

He came to his life's professional calling by happenstance. He was approaching college age when a boyhood friend, Denver Dickerson, told him, "Paul, why don't you come up to college and we'll try our hands at journalism?" At UNR, Professor Higginbotham pumped the newspaper gospel at the gangly youngster and Leonard soaked it up.

He was a young man blessed with maturity in his youth. At the Reno campus, he was a track star, the long-distance running ace of the era, and he was active in many organizations. But his greatest moment in life came at a campus dance when he met Gwenevere Frances Erikson. He would say years later, "I chased her 'til she caught me."

They married in 1938. This weekend, Gwen Leonard and I visited. She said of the man she'd been with for nearly fifty years, "His greatest attribute was that he was kind. He never really expected anyone ever to do him ill."

How fortunate all of us were to know such a person and to profit from his goodness!

Mary Gojack _____

MARY GOJACK was a rarity of rarities, a genuine original who truly did make a difference. She was a champion of the poor, of the underdog, of society's human doormats and of old people. She seemed the epitome of what Winston Churchill meant when he said, "You make a living by what you get, but you make a life by what you give." By the time Mary Gojack's life ended this week at the age of only forty-nine, she had made a great life by what she gave.

The former Nevada legislator and state pioneer of women's rights did not happen to espouse human rights, due process and responsible and responsive government by accident. She was born in Iowa, a fourth child. Her mother died of complications at Mary's birth. She was the daughter of a poor farmer, and she grew up in the Depression-wracked Midwest.

From her father, she was to acquire a curiosity about politics. Later, it would serve Nevadans well.

The work ethic that became her hallmark as Nevada legislator and activist seized her as a child. She was the girl baby-sitter, the teenage waitress, the youngster who earned pennies detasseling corn and doing small-town chores. Hillsboro, Iowa, where she grew up, was so tiny that only five were in her high school graduating class. Last August, ill with cancer, she went home again to her class reunion, which was an all-school, all-time rally that drew hundreds. Her classmates picked her as mistress of ceremonies.

The woman her Reno district sent to the legislature from 1972 through 1978 was a ring-wise and committed person. She was a paradox, for while she was voted in by the affluent southwest, she immediately went to do battle for the low-income have-nots. The people who year after year supported her weren't traditional party loyalists, but people who had no personal aspirations, who saw in her something that people are thirsting for—integrity. It was to her

lasting credit that after voters denied her quest for a role in Congress, she nonetheless maintained her network of supporters and friends.

In defeat, I thought of her as an even greater champion. There was the matter of her unpaid campaign costs after the losing effort against Paul Laxalt. Her Democratic party's effort to cover the debts fell leagues short. She and her remarkable husband, Robert Gorrell, would not permit one bill to go unpaid. They sold their own securities and whatever else was necessary to retire $120,000 in carry-over campaign debt. "To have done otherwise," notes her campaign manager and dear friend, Joan Kruse, "would have made Mary feel that she had betrayed those who had already contributed to her campaign."

Confronting her terminal illness was frightening, discouraging, painful. Yet, she seemed to those who saw her in the final months—and they numbered in the hundreds—stronger of will than ever. She was forthright and caring. The remarkable woman was showing the warmth that somehow did not come through clearly as a television campaigner. Critics had said she was a cold woman. She was completely the opposite.

Her laughter and presence lit up places and there was a streak of wit about her that never flagged. Even as she was hospitalized four days prior to her death, she was plotting to surprise daughter Pat Hixson with a newspaper ad on her thirtieth birthday. She counseled a friend whose marriage was on the rocks and hid a list of twenty tough-to-spell words that she had planned to spring on husband Bob during one of their spirited "My Word" contests. To the end, she clipped political stories from the *Gazette-Journal*, and when reporters called for insights into ongoing news stories, she summoned the strength to oblige them.

She had been a sentimental woman through her adult life, who cried easily, in anger and especially in frustration at any kind of injustice.

At the end of her life, she did not cry. She fretted somewhat jovially that the family's dachshunds, Minnie, Jennie and Kate, be well cared for. She fretted about things going right for "Bob and my kids." She worried about the things she did not get to do, including the book *Nevada Campaign* that she hoped to write. There was frustration that there were so many miles yet to travel. It was her way of saying that it is time to get on the road again, to complete un-finished business and to chart a new and better course.

Mary Gojack, rarity of rarities, one who left our place much better because she was here.

Reporter's Reporter

Gazette-Journal colleague Helen Manning died Monday and thus the career of an outstanding journalist ended too early. Helen had the talent and courage to be what so many of us in the newspaper business want to be, but cannot: a great reporter.

If you had plunked her down in a journalism lineup and challenged unknowing observers to "pick out the all-star," Helen wouldn't have been the choice on looks. Nature had shortchanged her on height; I doubt she ever weighed more than 100 pounds in her adult life; her manner of dress was dowdy; she was homely; she spoke only a decibel above a whisper. How deceiving appearances can be!

In her newspaper arsenal, Helen Manning had all the equipment that best serves the reader. Foremost was her absolute integrity. She earned a legion of critics during her career—they invariably were news sources bludgeoned by her intense questioning. But nobody ever charged her with intellectual dishonesty and made it stick.

She had a lot of things going for her. Thus did readers profit. She was intelligent; she was curious. Helen always had a nagging notion that a suspect was innocent, even after conviction; there was within her an ongoing hunch that establishment figures were unfairly punishing the little guys; if there was so much as an inch of crook in anybody on her news beat, she ultimately found it out; if she had an ego, she submerged it; she knew how to listen; she could not be intimidated; she had the stamina to wade into each tough newspaper day fresh and raring to go. Until her illness with cancer, she had never missed a day's work.

She was born Helen Edelstein and reared in a poor Jewish neighborhood in Los Angeles, the daughter of a mother who worked in the garment industry and a father who was a nonlawyer legal genius, who ultimately filed a brief that gave atomic spies Ethel and Julius Rosenberg a temporary stay of execution. The daughter, who was close to concert-pianist quality, elected journalism instead of music as a career. She majored in social studies at UCLA and became a diligent young reporter on the *Daily Bruin*, the campus newspaper.

She married young, had two children, and it wasn't a happy marriage. Helen Manning wound up with the kids and on welfare and ultimately turned to what would be her life's work and No. 1 love.

She first hired on with weeklies in Los Angeles, then apprenticed at a small daily in Hanford at the south end of San Joaquin Valley, and thence to the *Salinas Californian*, where she did distinguished work for fifteen years. It was in that rich agricultural setting that Helen covered the largest ongoing story of her career—the activities of César Chávez, his organizing of the United Farm Workers and the produce growers of the area.

Chávez once tried to hire her as his public relations woman, but she turned him down cold. "Daily journalism is my life," she said. Even while growers were grousing that Helen Manning's reporting was slanted toward Chávez, she exploded a story that tormented him and his organization—that his union's internal discipline practices were tantamount to a kangaroo court.

Her coverage in Salinas ran the whole spectrum: welfare, human interest, the hundreds of union stories, the courts. Eric Brazil, her former editor and closest friend, calls her the best reporter he's ever known.

She made her editors work because she didn't lob journalistic softballs across the news desk. Her stories were tough to edit, the result of her intense digging. If she had a fault, it was overwriting, the by-product of exhaustive interviews that were her hallmark.

There wasn't an inch of fake in her. She was blunt in her questioning. Her lack of personal tact was more upsetting to many sources than was the force of her inquiry. She didn't publicly trumpet that "the public has a right to know," but she believed it with religious fervor. Her last work, a series on the Greater Reno medical community, delved into how doctors look at themselves in terms of public responsibility and how medical people can improve their public image. It was not an easy series to explore under any circumstances and it was all the more difficult because Helen Manning, fifty-five, was dying.

She always had been one to do things on time, but in 1982 she had skipped her annual physical examination. Thus her cancer went undetected for too long. To the end, she did not cry about her fate. She regretted just one thing, she told several of us—that she could not be in Las Vegas covering the casino employees' strike.

Once a great reporter, always.

Woman of Distinction _____

NANCY SULLIVAN GOMES, frail now from her illness with cancer, stood there in the distinguished Nevadan spotlight on the Reno campus from which she had graduated.

The roar of the crowd engulfed her like a riptide; the love of her family and of her legion of friends overwhelmed and thrilled her. They were saying. "Thanks, Nancy, for all you've done for us."

Her school, the University of Nevada-Reno, traditionally bestows the Distinguished Nevadan citation at graduation time. But for Nancy Gomes, the honors were set early. She has fought the cancer since 1968. But it has spread. Her time is short.

She and the family left for Puerto Vallarta, Mexico, after the Distinguished Nevadan award event, to vacation. "The Mexican people, how wonderful they are; I spoke to them in my pidgin Mexican; my family kidded me that I was out on the beach, trying to organize the natives; when my family went out on buying sprees, I sang to them—'Look for the union label,'" laughed Mrs. Gomes.

This week, she returned home to Nevada, "The great old state, the one I've been so mad at at times, but my state, the only state I have."

From her Reno home, she reflected on her career, on her life, and on her Distinguished Nevadan designation.

"I thought I was too old to be thrilled. But really, when you know you're appreciated, it's marvelous. You know, I walked to a different beat, and yet they honored me. I was given these honors for things a lot of people did."

She spoke of her illness.

Detection in 1968; radical surgery in 1971. "Then when I was in the Nevada Legislature in 1977, I started feeling so sick, I couldn't believe it."

She spoke of her declining health: "Make every day count. If you want to do something, get on with it. That was a prime reason I

remained so active in this decade. I knew at some point, I wouldn't be too active."

Nancy Gomes, age fifty-two, activist, committed, never afraid of producing waves, has had a remarkable life. She never built a building or wrote a book, but she has erected a monument, Nevada-style, to herself with ideas and action.

She was born in Lovelock in 1926 and was influenced by the Great Depression ("Truly a great learning experience") and especially influenced by her mother, "who fed the have-nots until we ran out of food."

What has she done in her life? She prefers not to recount accomplishments. But from our memory, and our newspaper files, come these:

Social worker in rural Nevada; set up refugee program for Cuban families coming to Nevada in 1961; founded and directed the Foster Grandparent program at the then Nevada State Hospital; designed cottages for retarded children; initiated and lobbied for state legislation on public assistance, child welfare, adoption reform, initial Nevada Juvenile Code.

Consultant, Office of Economic Opportunity, U.S. Department of Health; wrote grants that were funded for operation in Washoe County, totaling $3.5 million; president of the League of Women Voters; author of publications on welfare, education, employment and community planning.

"Soroptimist Woman of the Year" in 1977.

Lobbyist who persuaded legislators that a cruel black market baby ring flourished in Nevada—the state wound up with one of the nation's strongest adoption laws; volunteer on environmental impact commissions and for the poor, the minorities, the aged and children.

Nancy Gomes's most remarkable commitment—"Make every day count"—was accelerated when she knew of her illness in 1968.

She became even more active.

She won election to the Washoe School Board in 1972.

Then she went after a Washoe assembly position. She campaigned hard. She stood up for education ("It covers a lot more than just blackboards") for old people ("Just talking about what ought to happen to the older citizen in Nevada isn't good enough").

She won a legislative seat and was a sure-fire bet for stardom until ill health hit her.

There are other accomplishments: leader of the Board of Equalization in Washoe; state treasurer of the Democratic party; and volunteer for many other worthy endeavors.

Her family—husband John Gomes of the U.S. Bureau of Mines and children Larry, Terry and Maryanne—she has loved above all.

She remains committed to the last. Too ill to do her own typing now, she is dictating stories on mental retardation in Nevada and on the legislature.

Nancy's sister, Leola Armstrong, seemed to summarize what Nancy Sullivan Gomes is when she nominated her for an honor: "She has never stopped working for her community and her state."

For these things, Nancy Gomes, and for many more, we thank you for all you've done for us.

·§·§·§·§·

Nancy Gomes died three months after "Woman of Distinction" was published. A Reno elementary school later was named after her.

It Was Meant to Be _____

THE NEWS STORY broke eighteen months ago. It was about an episode that carried all the potential for tragedy. Bill Pennington, chief executive officer of Reno Circus Circus, had been driving his powerboat at Lake Tahoe, and on that Saturday in June, it flipped and sank. Pennington went down with it.

But for a brave young California man, we would have been reporting that one of Nevada's best-known and ablest leaders was dead.

The rescuer's name was Gary Schmidt; he was nineteen, he lived in Hillsborough, south of San Francisco, and, as fate would have it, the day Bill Pennington and his boat went down, Gary Schmidt was nearby.

People immediately converged on the accident scene, saw that the boat driver was down with the craft and tried to reach him. All failed except one. Gary Schmidt kept diving. His lungs were bursting, but he finally got to the wreckage at an estimated depth of twenty feet. Schmidt saw Pennington trapped and somehow freed the unconscious executive. When they got Pennington to the surface, they first thought he was dead. No wonder. The man had been underwater for an estimated eight minutes. He wasn't dead but they already were speculating that he had suffered irreversible brain damage.

Gary Schmidt, son of a prominent San Francisco medical doctor, had left the accident scene after filing his report with the authorities. He said he had simply done what anybody would do: "A man was in jeopardy. I wanted to help."

Bill Pennington, deprived of oxygen for what would have been too long for most people, made a miraculous recovery. Days after the accident, when he could think and act, he directed: "We must find the youngster who saved me."

The trail quickly led to Schmidt. Not long out of high school, he had begun his education at the University of California at Berkeley,

and it seemed clear that with his academic credentials, his desire to achieve the best education possible and his own family's history of achievement the young man had a wonderful future.

Bill Pennington and Gary Schmidt came together and they clicked from that first moment. Pennington told me of their fast friendship the other day.

"I was three times Gary's age, yet there wasn't a gap there. Here was an intelligent young person, a motivated man, who had so much going for him. I learned that he was an ambitious youngster who loved school, who loved scholarship. Gary didn't have any vices."

The Nevadan, who has a personal fortune at his disposal, inquired whether he could reward the young Californian, but the boy, who grew up in one of the nation's most affluent communities, made it clear that having his new friend William Pennington alive and healthy was itself prime reward.

Someone told Pennington that Gary Schmidt loved cars, particularly sports cars.

Nine months ago, Bill Pennington bought his young friend a red Porsche convertible, costing in excess of $50,000. It wasn't simply a token of thanks. It was a gift to a dear new friend. The good-looking Schmidt was overwhelmed and in that soft-spoken way of his he said he was sincerely grateful.

Gary Schmidt, turned twenty, last summer traveled in Europe, came home to California and took up a new academic pursuit. He transferred from Cal-Berkeley to Stanford University, another of the world's great places of learning. There he would give that all-out commitment to the business administration field. The adrenaline had flowed in him that day at Lake Tahoe when he wouldn't quit diving. The same adrenaline pumped him up academically, making him want ultimately to excel as a professional person.

It was near the end of October and the youngster was settled in at the Stanford campus. On the eastern slope of the Sierra, Bill Pennington, sixty-two, flew out of Reno on a business trip.

Then came the call from his Circus Circus office to New York City. There had been an accident on California Freeway 280. The pavement was slick and wet and the hour late when a red Porsche crashed. When they got to Gary Schmidt, he was dead.

Bill Pennington immediately flew to California, crushed by the news about the youngster he had come to think of as another son.

Questions kept coming to him. Why this for Gary? Why the end of a promising young life? What if I hadn't given him the car? No one answered because no one knew. But Gary Schmidt's family spoke about the car. "Mr. Pennington, you must never feel guilt. It was meant to be."

At the funeral, the pastor asked people to speak of Gary Schmidt. It came Bill Pennington's turn. He rose and his grief choked off his words. But it was plainly evident, though the words could not come, that the man who was spared had come to love the one who died.

NEVADA
SPORTS

Football Memories ——————————————

IT IS THE SEASON of the audible, trap play, blitz, punt, passing pocket, strong or weak side, nose guard, prevent defense.

It is that three-month period when King Cliché spews: "Quick hands, great desire, winning in the trenches."

It is that September through November season when those who watch, and who play, are driven to frenzy by young men's insatiable appetites for yardage. Whether the land is attained by ground or by air, the struggle for terrain is apt to be fierce. As in actual war, it is the force that possesses the greatest power, intelligence and leadership that usually wins. But luck and especially superior commitment have been known to overcome a multitude of enemy strengths.

Football. What a marvelous and complicated game to watch. But to have played it is, I think, the greatest satisfaction. It makes little difference whether you languished in the obscurity of the interior line or whether you were the rare one who was Friday night's or Saturday's hero. When so many other life experiences fade, the football recollections burn vividly within you, as if your long ago yesterday is today.

Football playing memories revisited:

Season after season, that first practice day, the foremost autumn torment. Run, retch, run, barf. The lean players always out front, panting less, recovering faster. The muscles unstrained for the last nine months, refusing to obey the mind's commands. Aching lungs that provide less than required. Fat guys, finishing at the tail end of the wind sprints, amid the gulps for air, cursing themselves for ignoring coach's advice to "start your running early in the summer."

Football nomenclature changes. But football fundamentals are constant. Get in the best possible physical shape, then play beyond what your peak endurance will permit. Hit somebody as hard as you can, then hit harder. Intimidate, deceive and overpower somebody, and know that on the next play or next Saturday you may be the whipping boy.

It's really so simple. Be tougher than the enemy, know him better than he knows you, but know thyself, and ignore your own limitations.

The coaches' exhortations never change: "Get your butt down and keep it down; if I've told you once, I've told you a million times, hit 'em at the knees or ankles, not the neck; it's guys like you who don't pay attention who can lose for us next weekend; you better not miss practices if you expect to play on my ball club."

Football. Learning to do the unnatural—thrusting your body into swarms of other bodies; attempting top speed an instant after you were stationary; knocking people down; picking yourself up out of a thicket of legs, torsos, arms and elbows.

The quest for exquisite timing, the kind that springs eleven bodies into action in a moment. Endless practices, learning by rote, studying very few basic plays but countless variations of each basic play.

Football. No matter how many seasons you played, there was new knowledge required. Regardless of the same schools played again, they'd come at you with a fresh platoon of new talent and new devices. But always those familiar exhortations: "Give our passer more time, just four seconds, just give him that much; you've got to prove that you are more man than the other guy is; you've all got to concentrate on just one thing: winning."

From that eerie mood that gnaws at your gut before the kickoff to that wonderful first blow that wipes out your anxiety right down to the final gun, it's a wonderful game. It's the exhilaration of pushing and shoving and mauling and trying to prove domination over no more than 300 feet of ground. The great motivators: knowing that one of your failures can be disaster for everybody; knowing that the last guy you would let down is the teammate who relies on you; remember that when the coach talks to your squad, he's saying to each individual, "Play your hardest and do your best. If you do, you can live with yourself."

Young men will endure the tortures of the damned to say, "Yes, I play." Hip pointers, black and blue marks, spasms, fractures, cracked jaws, chipped teeth, mauled tendons, wrenched nerves and torn egos, all the products of collisions, intended or otherwise. All this to Win One for the Gipper, or for Reed High, or for the University of Nevada campus, north or south.

And then one day, when you are eighteen, or twenty-one or twenty-two if you play on to college, suddenly it's over. You're still at a tender age, but you've had it. Football's your past, not your future. And you know that nothing is quite so neglected in the spectator's memory as last season's senior. But it doesn't matter. What counts is that once upon a time you clawed for possession of a deviously shaped ball, so unpredictable in its bounce; that once you and your playing friends fought together for ten yards, as if playing was life's greatest mission.

Somehow as the years sweep past, with football memories still intact, you know that winning and losing taught you something immensely valuable.

So now you watch and occasionally you are asked, "You ever play football?"—and it feels good to say, "Yes, once upon a time."

The Lunatic Factory _____

JAMA ABDULLAHI SHURIYE strode into Reno's Mackay Stadium, which is halfway around the world from his home in Africa, and at first, it was so easy and logical—finding where to sit, I mean. He simply marched to Section B and plunked his slender body onto seat 4, row 5. Then came the hard stuff. For the next three hours, Jama tried to comprehend events of that Saturday afternoon. He was watching a peculiar American invention called football; it was the first time he had ever laid eyes on the sport, and for all the sense football made, he might just as well have been observing the she-nanigans in a lunatic factory.

This sport was crazy, complicated, so different from athletics at Jama's home in Mogadiscio, Somalia, hard by the Indian Ocean on the southeastern coast of Africa. In his country, where there is no television, soccer is the king of sports: eleven persons on each team; simple uniforms ("Shoes, socks, shorts and shirts") and the mission is to thrust a round ball ("Predictable in its bounce") into a small cubicle at either end of the field.

In his city, the capital of Somalia, Jama is director of planning for the Ministry of Higher Education and Culture. During this first visit to America, he is on the Nevada-Reno campus as an international administrative intern. He is a happy and articulate man and a careful listener. But understand football?

Jama stared at the weirdly dressed players during pregame warm-up. Poor deformed young men with lumps rising off their shoulders and bulges at their thighs. Above their hunched backs perched the helmets. The steel bars, sheltering their young faces, made it impossible to observe their features. They wore pants, but the garments were ridiculous, being cut off at the knees. At either end of the field rose white poles, with a single horizontal pole suspended in midair. And as 1 P.M. approached, small airplanes circled above, and people jumped out and floated into Mackay Stadium. "What positions do the parachutists play? Ah, this must be the famous American football aerial attack."

Football—game of contradictory terms. It is called a pigskin, Jama is told, but it isn't made of pigskin. The sport is called football, yet only occasionally are the feet put to the ball.

Contradictions: the "gentle" Americans, seated all around Jama, scream, "Kill the referee." Back home during soccer games, when the crowd says kill, it means it. Yet here, Jama witnesses no referee's blood, and he sees no knives, guns, not even a lynching rope. Spectators are here to watch, yet many listen to what they are seeing on their hand-held radios. How very quaint!

The game begins.

In the seat next to Jama, UNR's dean of education, Ed Cain, attempts to explain. It isn't easy.

Jama is horrified. Such mayhem, such collisions of the young bodies. The players assault each other at full speed. Football seems to him such a very rough game—heavy bodies, sometimes as many as seven or eight, land atop the poor man holding the strange oblong ball. Why is it that at times the teams have three plays and then kick, but in other instances they are permitted to play without the kicks? Strangest of all—Jama sees a large man crouch over the ball. Another player walks up behind and puts his hand under his teammate's hindquarters? How very unusual.

If the poles at either end of the field are so important, why aren't they put into use more often? Why, without warning, are all the players withdrawn from combat, to be replaced by brand-new player units? Why is it that the players cheer and wave their arms right after they are battered by the people of the other team? With such outright physical violence, why aren't more players injured? Why do the men in the black and white uniforms not take more care to keep their handkerchiefs in their pockets? Is there no discipline to this game of football? The new players don't even bother to report their jersey numerals to the referees!

Much of the time the players just stand around in a circle, whispering. Why?

Now the players in the blue and white uniforms are permitted to keep the ball and they push the enemy back, back, and the spectators are on their feet, cheering. Then the UNR team pushes the ball past the final white stripe. A cannon roars to Jama's left. He hopes nobody was injured by the blast.

Finally, the football game ends. Jama walks with his American friends to the exit. It has been very confusing. He glances to his left, just before departing the stadium, and is told that just west is the UNR Booster parking lot. Jama sees spread before him the most confusing scene of all—a small sea of camper trucks and mobile dwellings. Funny people, these Americans. Why in the world would they drive their houses to a football game?

Football Shoes _____

THE FOOTBALL SHOES were most unusual, as was the remarkable young player who wore them.

There was no way on God's green earth that Don Ferguson should have been playing high school football. He was crippled, and crippled boys aren't supposed to run and block and tackle. But he did.

Don Ferguson died in Elko last week at the age of forty-eight after more than a year's illness with cancer. When the news came, my mind filled with memories of thirty years ago. The pictures are vivid. Pictures of courage do not vanish easily, if ever.

We had been close friends as schoolboys in Fallon and we were football teammates for three seasons, playing side by side in the line. Together, as underclassmen, we tried to earn regular playing status. It was easier for me because I had two good legs. Don had one good one. Yet, we became starters the same year.

Don's left leg was smaller and lame and he was slower than the others and in the dressing room we could see that his left foot was misshapen. We never asked, and Don did not talk about it, but it was said out of his presence that he had had polio.

In fact, when he was eight, Ethel and Lawrence Ferguson and their four sons lived at Round Mountain in Central Nevada. Don took sick with the chills and fever and his parents took him to Tonopah. The doctor thought it was a passing childhood illness. It wasn't. He spent his ninth birthday at Washoe Medical Center in Reno, where he was a patient for eight months, undergoing therapy.

Oh, sure, he would be able to limp through life. But as for hard physical work and especially sports, they were out of the question. Or so the doctors thought.

Don was a prodigious worker as a teenager on his parents' Fallon ranch, and in later life in ranching and in construction. He hurt a lot, but he never complained about the trick fate pulled on him.

Playing football with him convinced all of us what a great boy he was, and what a man he would become.

Don Ferguson was a six-footer and his playing weight was around 205 pounds. Ranch work made him powerful from the waist up.

But because of the twisted foot, he couldn't wear football shoes. The rest of us wore the conventional cleated shoes. Don wore brown work boots, laced to just above his ankles, and he could no more dig into turf than he could run. But he ran and he dug in.

His special football shoes were commonplace to the rest of us and we paid them no mind. But the games were something else. He played guard on defense and, in those early moments at the scrimmage line, I remember that rival players would do a double take. "What's this? Truly this is a Fallon farm boy who wore his clodhoppers to play us!" He heard snickers and occasionally saw a pointed finger.

The laughs didn't last long. If you ran straight at Ferguson, you were punished. Our tackles and ends, aware of Don's slowness, protected his flanks. He protected his own assigned turf.

Nobody ever protected a territory so well, against such odds, as the boy with the unusual football shoes.

Unusual shoes. Extraordinary man.

Basketball Memories _____

IT IS LATE AFTERNOON and they take their postgame stroll into the
Reno Elks Lodge, fresh from their demolition of St. Mary's College; athlete-heroes who are in their teens or early twenties; the
Wolf Pack, our players of the hour, champions without a pennant;
the most exciting Nevada-Reno basketball chaps since Jake Lawlor's
1946–47 wonder men.

Before dusk comes to end this gloriously sunny day, they will
learn that a twenty-victory season was, indeed, enough to win them
tournament favor. In another seventy-two hours, they will be at
Corvallis, Oregon, in a hostile arena, playing hometown Oregon
State, and the pressure will be on again. But for now, they relax,
savor this moment, soak up fan affection.

It is a special pleasure at this public reception to see these boys up
close after months of watching from afar at Centennial Coliseum.

Dapper Johnny High arrives at the Elks Lodge decked out in a
tuxedo, oozing class; Edgar Jones is a gentle giant, dispensing his
signature to the swarms of children; Stevie Hunter has the striking
good looks of a black Valentino; the charismatic Thaxter Arterberry
is the most articulate of a quiet bunch at the microphone; the pride
of Carson City, Mike Longero, asked to say something, says only,
"Something." The scoring machine, Howard "Fly" Gray, appears
frail in street clothes; the massive Alvin Alexander has muscles atop
muscles. Absent are the inspirational and unsung Mike Stallings and
that dribbler-whiz Raul Contreras, both presumably back on campus studying. Reserves Dale Wilson and Aaron Cusic join in the
pleasure of giving autographs.

Fan adulation is not confined to children. The elders paw at the
Nevada stars, grip their hands, lead standing ovations, of which
there are plenty, into the early evening. The players eat it up. They
love it, they deserve it.

Jim Carey, the coach, the architect of all this, is numb with the thrill of the tournament confirmation. He has steeled himself to hear bad news. When it is good, he brushes away happy tears. He provides the classiest touches at a classy postgame program, overlooking no one and introducing his wife as the greatest person he's ever known.

But it is the players who are kept in the spotlight. They have been a remarkable crew at Nevada-Reno; not a big team as collegians go these days, but intense, quick, unpredictable; capable of a comeback, or of snatching defeat from the jaws of victory; always exciting whether they're cold or hot, a collection of memorable individuals, yet a cohesive team.

The thing this Nevada team was most adept at was providing lasting memories, mostly sweet.

Thanks to Carey and his team for the memories.

Jake Lawlor _____

REMEMBERING Jake Lawlor, the Nevada coach we hated to love, but did. Jake has died. But the memory of him is thriving. He was tormentor, intimidator, agitator. He was inspirational and he was his athletes' leader, brother and father-confessor.

Take any sport at any season's opening practice. Jake was ready for his sermon. His fixed stare stabbed us like tracer bullets. He spit verbal gravel. The words always were the same: "You are my squad. I am interested in your welfare, your improvement. I am interested in you winning your share. Hopefully, more than your share."

His players prayed they would receive his tongue-lashings. If they didn't, it meant they wouldn't play. To defy him was curtains. To please him totally was impossible.

Jake Lawlor had heard a rumor that there was athletic perfection but, to him, that's all it was. Idle rumor. He wouldn't waste his time on anybody who couldn't produce for the team.

"If you lose, I don't want you walking off with your tail between your legs. Get your head up. But dammit, don't lose!"

He preached constantly that the grass wasn't greener on the other side. Once he won us over, he could do things and say things that few, if any, coaches could get by with. He thought a psychologist was crazy for suggesting that a naughty child be spanked long after the crime. He paddled our butts *now*. He hated recruiting with a passion. To him, it was castor oil, because it might mean coddling a pampered athlete, or his doting parent.

It has been twenty-six years since I last played on a Jake Lawlor team, but his words are as clear as if I had heard them this morning: "If you can't cut it, get out!"

He was a ferocious brawler when he played and in his salad days he was no teetotaler.

It made no difference whether he coached grammar school kids, preps, collegians or future professionals. He drove them, whipped

them. He was a relentless tyrant. His face flowered into tomato red and his hot words stung. Somehow, through his hysterics, every player knew he was a textbook case of self-discipline and that he didn't hate us. He loved us.

Years later, I discovered that he wasn't a genius concerning our names, our parents' names and our family trees. He kept a book on every squad, from his first coaching season in 1932. He memorized details about the most obscure squad member. He kept reviewing them after a long-ago season. "I never want to embarrass a boy by forgetting him," he declared.

His anger was never faked. He couldn't say to a boy, "Now, son, come over here. This is the way you should be doing it." He roared, blasted, ripped and tore at our deficiencies: "In fifty years, I doubt you'll amount to anything. Wake up. You better quit letting your teammates down."

Jake was Irish and he didn't worry about much. He wasn't a neurotic loser and he never had an ulcer and he didn't hold postdefeat grudges.

He never had much trouble with parents. They knew he never had the intention of hurting a youngster. He could go beyond enthusiasm. What I mean is, he could be wild, yet he was controlled. He knew where the ball was, why it wasn't where he wanted it, who was dogging it, who wasn't in physical shape. God, he knew everything. He could stare inside your mind and read you and he somehow could make players believe they had more potential than truly existed.

Jake Lawlor never criticized a player publicly. He didn't wash his linen in the media, he never boasted when his team won, and he never gave an alibi when he lost. He was tough to interview. As verbal as he was in practice and during games, he could be a clam during a news interview. He said of the media, "It's nice to have them on your side, and it's hell when they're not."

He was the godfather of more than thirty youngsters, all born to those he had coached. Would you ask a man you didn't like to be your kid's other father? Hardly. That was reserved for the man we loved.

Jake Lawlor.

Jimmie Olivas Returns ──────────

SURE THINGS: the sun rises and sets; Old Faithful blows its top; the Pacific whales migrate; swallows find Capistrano; the salmon swim upstream; ocean tides come then depart on schedule. Jimmie Olivas returns for another University of Nevada-Reno boxing season.

Olivas, unique, unforgettable and as consistent a part of the UNR campus scene as the Mackay Statue, is back for his thirtieth season as Wolf Pack boxing coach, and his results are predictable: he will teach his young men to fight and win. He will entertain them with his notoriously flawed memory, tickle them with an eloquence easily as tangled as that of Casey Stengel; they will go away after the final bell, singing his praise, and they will never forget him.

Olivas's craggy face looks like it suffered a losing war with a baby tank. The furrowed brow and dented nose and the faint scars of his own young ring wars make him appear hostile. Under that gruffness beats a heart as big as all outdoors. His voice is a rasp. His memory, especially of names, makes any absentminded professor seem a whiz by comparison.

He is competitive and fiery. He baits referees with the best of baiters and is not quick to forgive the judge who votes against a Nevada boxer in a close bout. I have been watching and admiring Jimmie Olivas since 1950, the year he became Nevada's coach. Never have I seen him fail to back his men to the hilt. He never knowingly overmatches his boxers. Their safety always has been uppermost with him.

Olivas came to Reno from Los Angeles in 1929 as a teenager. In UNR's 1930 yearbook, he is a curly-haired, smiling youngster, staring off a page reserved for members of Sigma Alpha Epsilon fraternity. Boxing was considered a minor sport in those years, but Olivas was a Major-Leaguer, a tough 147-pounder.

He became coach three decades ago, following the departure of Cliff Devine.

Talk about staying power! When Olivas took over, Truman was president, Dr. Malcolm Love was UNR president and there was a war going on in Korea. Olivas has survived a parade of coaches who have come and gone through the revolving athletic door. He has fought off attempts to kill and bury college boxing. Always a great teacher, he has produced national and regional champions. But to him, the lesser-skilled boys are every bit as important.

Olivas is a genius at teaching fundamentals. In a sport that requires tremendous stamina, he pushes and shoves and nags his men into top physical condition. If a young man is coachable and has heart, he has a chance to be a champion under this coach.

The ultimate testimony to Jimmie Olivas's ability is the result obtained.

His boxers do not fall into trouble with the law. They do not keep the headline writers busy with tales of misbehavior. They are not campus troublemakers. There is an unbeatable kinship in boxing, and Olivas's team members remain friends forever. It is a rare day when one of his men is academically ineligible.

Jimmie Olivas, gruff and gracious, incapable of giving anything less than the fullest support to his men, is the senior boxing coach on the American college scene. In his thirty Nevada seasons, he has coached hundreds of youngsters. I have never known one of them to knock him. I have never known one of them who wouldn't confess love for him.

Coach Jimmie. What a man!

An Idol, Jack Dempsey, Dies _____

WHEN I WAS growing up, my father, every day or so, would bring up Jack Dempsey's name. Dad would crouch there in our little house, bob and weave, crashing hooks and undercuts on an imaginary enemy, and say, "This was Jack's style, son. He was the greatest of our champions."

Dad's sermons about the mighty world champion soaked in like the Good Book. God and Dempsey were supreme. My father had grown up with Dempsey on everyone's mind. Like millions, he was a disciple and, like the others, he passed the legend on to his son.

Jack Dempsey's death last week stirred these memories and many more. When I was a kid and Dad was urging me to be tough, like Dempsey, I never dreamed I'd ever meet the Great One. When you're little and have no notion of the promise of tomorrow, you dare not hope to touch a human god, let alone speak to one.

Then fate brought me into journalism. I had a chance to grow, to learn, to explore. I gained, in my newspaper work, a chance to travel new highways and get acquainted with magnificent travelers along the way.

One whom I met several times was Jack Dempsey. I have never been ill at ease in the presence of the famed. Quite the opposite. Relaxation with the high and the mighty is something the Big Ones appreciate. But with Dempsey, I was something else. Expecting to be dismissed quickly. Nervous. But with the champ, there was no need. He was as comfortable as worn shoes, as playful as a basket of puppies. That he was as famous as any American never turned his head or diluted his sensitivity to those who approached him.

I first met the champion in Reno in October 1964. I had by then graduated from sportswriting and was a young editor. But I kept getting back to writing and when I heard Dempsey had returned to Reno, where he'd spent much time in the 1930s and 1940s, I had to get an interview. It was one of the easiest I ever arranged. Dempsey was staying at a motel on South Center Street. I called. I had heard that his voice was high-pitched. Indeed it was, and when he came on the line I had to stop short of asking, "Are you certain this is Mr. Dempsey?"

Dempsey had charm. On my end of the line was still another of the thousands of awestruck fans. He put me at ease fast. "Love to visit you, friend. You meet me here and we'll take a little walk together."

He had on a white shirt, a plaid jacket, pants and a belt buckle with a big engraved "D" on it. We chatted idly, he taking the lead. "Yes," he confirmed, "I am in town to see longtime Nevada friends Bill Graham and Maisie and Vinton Muller and to convalesce from an illness that has nagged me."

We walked to Powning Park across from the Riverside Hotel. My photographer friend Don Dondero joined us and snapped photos as I sat with Dempsey on a bench while interviewing him. A Reno old-timer walked past. He did a double take and nearly had a stroke on the spot. He was seeing the man who pulverized anything that stood in his boxing way, the man who could lick our old man. After the interview during which I had my picture taken with Jack Dempsey, I called my father and shared the amazing news. "Dad, your idol and mine was in town. Dempsey. Yeah, and he was such a wonderful person." My dad had to have a picture and he got it. Pronto!

Our paths crossed a few more times. I would go to New York City, walk on Broadway near the theater district, go directly to the famous Jack Dempsey Restaurant. Peeking into that big plate-glass window out front, I'd see the champ, talking or listening, hands usually gesturing, as if he was flailing somebody. Twice I walked in, and both times Dempsey pretended he remembered me. He was not only a great fighter, but a superb actor. "Yeah, yeah, sure, Reno a few years ago, right?"

Always, my eyes traveled his face for signs of the combat he was famous for. There was the scar tissue and a slightly bent ear. The gesturing hands. Silver streaked his hair.

In 1975, on a newspaper trip to the Big Apple, I tried desperately to get to Dempsey for one last interview. He by then had been forced to close his restaurant.

And he had finished his biography. I used contacts, got his phone number, but I couldn't get past his housekeeper, who shielded him more effectively than any great boxing trainer. "Mr. Dempsey just isn't up to an interview." That was it.

When he died, I joined millions who said, "A part of my own living history is gone." We retain the memory, though. Nothing is finer than remembering a champion who was a true champion.

GLIMPSES
OF THE
FAMOUS

Meeting Patrick McCarran _____

I GOT MY FIRST LOOK at a U.S. senator when I was sixteen and swore I must be squinting smack into the face of God Himself. I was then an apprentice printer at the weekly *Fallon Standard*. The year was 1948 and my bosses were the *Standard*'s incomparable owner-editor, Claude H. Smith, and an outstanding all-around newspaperman, Ken Ingram. It was summer. I was working full-time.

These were pretelevision days in Nevada, so any glimpse one got of the high and mighty was provided by printed words, or via radio or in the flesh. I had read much about Patrick McCarran, the famed Nevada Democrat, and my elders assured me that indeed the great one would occasionally bless our Fallon, small as it was, with his presence.

I had no comprehension of the real Nevada, its rural political power (reapportionment?—what was that?), nor of how much politicians loved to move among the natives. My doubts vanished when I came face to face with Senator McCarran.

As I remember, our band of printers and front office people at the *Standard* knew in advance of the senator's visit. In those days, so-called advance notice consisted of a friendly phone call: "Hello, Claude Smith, this is Pat. I'll be coming your way tomorrow and I'd like to stop by and pay my respects."

I don't recall at what hour McCarran arrived at our building on Center Street. Whatever—I kept eyeballing the front office—waiting for my first look at a statesman.

Then, without the roll of drums, minus the brass band or any public display whatever, there he was!

It was editor Smith's custom to bring some visitors through our building and introduce them to employees. Instead, on the occasion of McCarran's appearance, the senator and his hosts stayed up front. I faked looking productive in the back room, but spent maybe a half-hour furtively inspecting the proceedings up front.

The senator and Smith chatted amicably. Smith loved a political subject above any other. When a customer or news source visited, the boss would introduce McCarran, then lay back, chain-smoke and enjoy the pleasant surprise of those encountering the Great One.

I had work to do in our basement and the only route was through the front office. I was paralyzed at the prospect of facing the author of the McCarran Act, the man who had blown the whistle on Franklin Roosevelt when he tried to pack the U.S. Supreme Court. What could a schoolboy possibly say to the famous one? I knew for certain that the boss would stop me en route downstairs. He did.

"Hold on," Smith said, catching me by the arm. "Shake hands with Senator McCarran." Up close now, I was surprised that McCarran was a stocky man—why, I was taller! He had a massive head, topped by a shock of totally gray hair. He looked every bit the elder statesman. The senator was dressed to the teeth that day. He wore a handsome dark blue suit, a white shirt, a matching tie and shoes polished so brightly they could have been used as mirrors.

I was quaking, my mouth feeling full of cotton, and I could hardly muster a simple "Hello." McCarran stuck out a firm hand, pumped mine and made me feel he was the one truly charmed at meeting me. My conversation with the noted visitor couldn't have lasted more than a minute. In that twinkling, Patrick McCarran commanded my awestruck attention; he managed to extract from me the size of Fallon High School's student body, my age, whether I played football and what I wanted to be when I grew up.

It was sixty seconds of being with a superstar! To the senator, I was simply another person to charm. For the teenage boy, it was a moment to talk about for weeks. And to remember for a lifetime.

President Carter _____

WASHINGTON, D.C.— It is an overcast but pleasant winter afternoon, with but a hint of breeze nudging Washington.

Large buses are parked alongside the Capital Hilton Hotel, where we are staying, and they spew diesel fumes onto a street crowded with cars and scurrying pedestrians. As we step aboard, our drivers appear bored. For them, it's to be another short haul, another day, another dollar. But for the 150 riders, all of them Gannett newspaper people, including 6 from Reno, the next two hours will be special. They feel anticipation. For a large percentage, there will be the experience of seeing an American president in the flesh for the first time.

We are transported to the old Executive Office Building, alongside the White House. There, the waiting starts. We line up. It is slow going through security's checkpoint. Guards work from an advance list of visitors. Each of us is asked to show identification, including a photograph. For those from Nevada, it's a snap, with our portraits on driver's licenses. Not so easy for one man, an Arizonan, who has left his wallet at the hotel. A spokesman for our group vouches for him and he is passed through.

An elevator, taking clusters of up to ten, hauls us to the third floor. Women employees guide us to a room. We take to folding chairs, awaiting the individual appearances of first Henry Schlessinger, the energy czar, then Carter, the president, followed by Kahn, the inflation fighter.

Schlessinger appears first. Square of jaw, graying; red-complexioned. He addresses himself exclusively to the energy topic, and the message seems more ominous when heard in person than when seen in print. "We've got plenty of troubles. The Iranian situation bodes ill with respect to energy. The world is gobbling up oil and gas much faster than it can be found."

Last comes Kahn, the former college economics professor. His is a grim task of leading the anti-inflation charge. Kahn is humorous, considering his onerous goal. He spews one-liners and poses questions that he himself answers. The audience roars. Kahn, for all his mirth, picks and chooses his words with care. Pencils are flashing onto notepaper. Just to make certain of documentation, whirring government tapes are logging all words uttered by our three speakers. Kahn's visit is funny, informative and brief.

It is the middle speaker, Carter, who most intrigues us.

Schlessinger is gone now. We remain seated. Prior to the president's entry, a Secret Service man glides unobtrusively on the balcony above us. He peers down, eyes darting through the seated crowd. Another agent, battery-operated walkie-talkie strapped to his waist, glides around the audience, surveying. The time must be near for Carter's entrance.

On the first balcony above us, and to our right, four Secret Service men appear quietly. Another is above us and watching from behind. On our ground level, a woman agent glides quietly to our left, near the draped windows that look out over the Washington Monument.

At 2:05 P.M. deputy press secretary Walter Wurfel puts the presidential seal on the rostrum's front side. Carter enters. Everyone rises. The president is smiling. He glides easily to the front, watched by all eyes save those of the Secret Service: the president shakes hands with the ten people in the front row. He steps to the podium and speaks softly into three microphones.

He looks older than on television, Reno's Larry Gasho will remember. Jim Rowley, another Reno man, is getting his first look at a president. He wants to reach inside his coat and fetch a pen. But Rowley imagines that the two stern agents who walked in with the president and now are set about seven feet to either side of Carter are eyeballing him. Rowley doesn't move a muscle. Warren Lerude, the Reno publisher, is seeing his fourth president, Carter, for the first time. He notes the sparkle in Jimmy Carter's eyes, the speaker's slow-paced, southern-laced manner of speaking, and yet Carter's quick movement from topic to topic.

Reno's Robert Wingard will always remember the up-front security. The agent to Carter's right, vigilant, his gaze darting here, there, everywhere. The other security man, bulkier than the first, giving off a powerful "don't try anything" glare.

Carter has a crowded agenda this day. Yet, he seems unhurried.

He can't answer one question and admits he doesn't know. He says, "Presidents aren't omnipotent, as you may already have heard." The newspaper people laugh.

I had seen Carter once before, eight months ago, at a Gridiron Dinner. Today, he has grown markedly older. He is trim, as always: but the face is weary, the skin at the neck is loose and appears more aged. There is no makeup for TV this day—just the president, as he really is. I remember thinking again what a toll the stress of the office takes on all its occupants.

The president has few comments prepared. He mentions a freedom of the press case, in which the administration supports us.

The questions come. Carter responds, his right hand gesturing at chest level for emphasis. His left flashes up occasionally and you can see the gold wedding band his wife Rosalynn gave him.

The tape recorders get down everything, watched by women attendants who never remove their eyes from them. Carter's time with us is at an end. It is 2:25 P.M.

"Have a nice day, everybody," he says.

Everyone rises. Carter glides to the exit, shaking hands here and there.

He is flanked by the two agents, with others bringing up the rear.

Everyone is watching the president as he leaves. All except his aides. They are still watching us, safeguarding their man.

Then they are gone.

Phyllis Diller's Advice _____

WASHINGTON —Bob Cashell and his wife Nancy had just attended their first state dinner at the White House. The event honored the president of Austria.

The Cashells returned to their hotel, the Hay Adams.

"Hey, Nancy, let's have a drink before turning in."

"OK, Bob."

Into the Hay Adams bar they went, took a seat and ordered a drink. They were the only customers. It was close to midnight.

They soon had company.

In strode a woman and her escort.

The Cashells didn't know the man, but they instantly recognized the woman.

Phyllis Diller.

"Let's introduce ourselves," suggested Cashell, never known for shyness.

"OK."

Comedienne Diller and her friend, Howard Rose, greeted the Nevadans warmly.

"Please join us."

"OK."

Each couple quickly learned the other also had been at the White House event. That speeded the togetherness.

Diller began her interview of Bob Cashell.

"So you live in Nevada? What do you do out there?"

"Well, we operate hotel-casinos in Reno and Winnemucca."

"You also involved in politics?" Diller inquired.

"Yes."

"How so?"

"I'm lieutenant governor of Nevada."

"Well, what do you want to do politically after you grow up?" Diller asked.

"Well, being Nevada governor would be appealing."

"Well let me tell you, Bob," said Diller, "I've got advice that could help you."

"What's that?"

"I think you ought to get a nose job. I mean really get the old proboscis amended. Howard Rose here, he listened to me and had his nose rebuilt. Didn't you, Howard?"

"I sure did. Phyllis told me it wouldn't hurt a bit, so I came out of the surgery hurting, and all black and blue. I was so upset I could have punched her lights out."

"Anyway, Bob," Diller continued, "get your nose done!"

"OK."

"Another thing. You need a face lift. Real bad."

Cashell gulped.

"I've had eight lifts. Works every time," Diller volunteered. "For a while."

"Is that all there is to it? I just go and get a lift?" Cashell asked.

"No," Diller said. "First you ought to lose sixty pounds. You're simply too fat now to run for governor."

"OK."

"Lose the weight, then get the face lift. Otherwise, getting the lift first, then losing the weight, you might have to have another lift, and another, and another . . . Who knows, you might exceed my record of eight."

"OK."

"There's further proof that plastic surgery makes you look younger," she said. "Consider Howard again. He's had a ton of face lifts and just look what it's done for him! Howard, I think you look great for a man who's 108."

Diller surrendered the name of her plastic surgeon to Cashell. He took notes.

Dinner with Mr. Vice-President _____

I TELEPHONED HOME from my office around mid-morning Thursday and asked my wife Marilyn if everything was shaping up all right for our dinner party that night for Vice-President George Bush.

"So, what's happening?" I led off.

"Oh, not much, Rollan. I'm just standing here talking to a Secret Service man while I fold my clothes."

I mean, it was that kind of week. Very different.

This year, Bush is making 137 appearances in 33 states, stumping for fellow Republicans. Thursday's reception-dinner at our home was such a stopover.

I have no appetite to be a political partisan. But Jim Santini called me six weeks ago and asked if we would host an event for George Bush. When the vice-president of the United States wants to come calling, one seems compelled to be polite. I answered yes.

With that background explained, let me share some details of Bush's visit with us.

For those wondering whether security is tight around the vice-president, the answer is a resounding yes. Bush's advance party and his Secret Service detail began to brief us at our house a week ago. With a heavy dose of help from Nevada law enforcement, most particularly the Reno Police Department, the Secret Service tossed up an early protective net.

Agents poked, prodded and probed the Melton home and yard in advance of, and during, the Bush visit. A highly trained dog, guided by the gentle voice signals of his trainer, sniffed through every nook and cranny early on, for a hint of untoward chemicals or explosive devices.

Approximately forty Secret Service agents—men and women— were on duty in Reno during Bush's visit, and perhaps two-thirds of them collected at our place, where eighty-nine guests turned out to greet our notable visitor.

The security nerve center was actually a command post at Reno's Airport Plaza. Orchestrating the intricate show was veteran Secret Service agent Steve Burau, thirty-six, a 1972 graduate of the University of Nevada-Reno. He is the son of Douglas Burau, of Reno, a retired FBI agent.

Agents installed four special phones in our house before the visit, linking themselves to the White House, to Air Force Two, in which the vice-president flies, and to other places. Reno's fire marshal had visited us earlier, too, telling us to lay in additional fire extinguishers, just in case.

Thursday turned out to be cold, causing Marilyn to joke, "Looks like God is no Republican today." But the weather was the only "downer" in our memorable event. Bush, a fellow with great presence, waded into the crowd, pressing the flesh. Nearby, bartender Lorene Sullivan fixed a vodka martini, with four olives, for "a guy with a wire sticking out his ear." The Secret Service agent handed the drink to Bush.

One of the free world's finest caterers, Judy Buckingham, had her crew doing a classy job; chef Jack Baxley cooked the beef just right; the wine flowed at a steady clip; the man who wants to succeed Ronald Reagan table-hopped.

When Bush reached a table of eight where Reno's Tom Reviglio sat, the Nevadan glanced up at the tall, lean vice-president, gestured to an empty chair and said, "Have a seat, Stud!" Bush laughed. Reviglio pressed on, noting Bush's tie clasp, its presidential seal glistening. "If you start living at the White House, will you give me one of those clips?" But Bush answered, "Why wait?" He took off the clip and gave it to the Nevadan. Like I said, it was an unusual event.

I guided the guest of honor to each of the nine tables during the dining and he visited each for about five minutes. Then Bush spoke briefly, urging the party faithful to help Santini become U.S. Senate successor to Paul Laxalt. His comments followed a second encounter with the irrepressible Tom Reviglio, who told Bush, "I like you, and wish you well, but I want Paul Laxalt in the White House."

Then the early favorite for the 1988 presidential nomination took off to the airport for a flight to Colorado Springs. With him went his cadre of staff and Secret Service.

The Nevada guests lingered awhile, sharing tales of the night.

Then everyone was gone, leaving us with good memories about a week that was—to say the least—unique.

FAITH
HOPE AND
CHARITY

Town Without Strangers _____

CATHERINE BEARER lay in agony on the wet highway and she cried out for her two babies and she tried to go to them but the officers held her down.

Minutes earlier, they had gotten their groceries at the Del Monte Shopping Center. They had started back across rain-splattered, four-lane Highway 395 to their $55-a-week motel room. Catherine saw the truck rushing at them from the darkness, but it was too late. They were hit.

Now, twenty-seven-year-old Catherine Bearer struggled and called out their names. But Amy Marie Barr, eight, and Cathy Lin Barr, two, were under the sheets nearby, crushed.

She had gone through hell all her life, it seemed. She grew up poor in St. Mary's, a small town in northwestern Pennsylvania. She dropped out of school when she was a high school junior and was married at eighteen. She had two miscarriages, then Amy was born in 1971. A son died two days after birth. There followed two additional miscarriages. Then Cathy came in 1977. Not long afterward, the children's father, James Barr, said he was going to town for a while. He never came back.

She married a second time, but it didn't work out. Afterward, she worked at whatever she could find: maid, waitress, store clerk. Without an education, she found opportunities severely limited. Her parents, the Bobenrieths, helped as best they could. She had her daughters. That was what counted most.

Catherine was sick of St. Mary's, with its limited chances, its ex-husbands, its carbon factories and its prejudice toward fat people. She is tall and heavy and she was discouraged and she needed a change of scenery. Six weeks ago, Catherine, a girl friend and Amy and Cathy piled into Catherine's rattletrap car and lugged what little they owned across America. They stopped briefly in Reno, long enough to learn that the place was booming. They drove on to San

215

Francisco to visit Catherine's brother, William Bobenrieth. He was tending to his eight children. His wife is institutionalized. So Catherine decided to double back to Reno. She and the daughters arrived on February 8. She continued looking for a job until the accident eleven days later.

Here she was, 2,800 miles from home, her daughters dead, nothing left for her but despair, alone in a town of strangers, "a cold, gambling town," she had heard. She was in the third-floor room at Washoe Medical Center, a woman crying, unable to see without the glasses that were smashed that night. She was bruised from head to toe, but there were no broken bones. Her mother, Mary Bobenrieth, sixty-one, had driven thirty-six hours straight from Pennsylvania to be with her. Her brother William came from San Francisco, his eight children with him.

The newspapers and radio and television told what happened and strangers rallied. Ruth Lobb of Reno read that Mrs. Bearer was from Pennsylvania, Mrs. Lobb's native state, and she was the first to visit. A Lovelock couple collected $75 and drove to Reno and gave it to Catherine Bearer. Reno optician Walt Immers, calling through the night, managed to fill her prescription so she could see her daughters' funeral. Sympathetic northern Nevadans flooded her hospital room with so many calls they had to be cut off so she could get some sleep. A Reno resident, Shelley Swalwinski, asked Nevada National Bank to act as repository for the Catherine Bearer Fund. The bank instantly set up an account. Gifts have ranged from $2 to $200. Three days ago, a Reno man handed Catherine Bearer a check for $750, more money than she ever saw in a lump. She cried.

She was discharged from Washoe Medical Center and she and her mother went to K-Mart and bought little lavender dresses for the joint funeral. The service was held at Reno's Little Flower Catholic Church. A choir of children sang. The young priest told of the devastated mother's faith. A small cluster of family clung to each other and wept and the priest read from Catherine Bearer's handwritten note, jotted down on Motel 6 stationery: "So remember my children with joy and happiness, for if you can only remember them with tears and sadness, don't remember them at all."

A small procession went to Mountain View Cemetery and Amy and Cathy Barr were buried in caskets donated by O'Brien's Funeral Home.

Catherine Bearer will not leave the warm and supportive town where her girls are buried. Nor will her brother, William Boben-rieth. He got a job at J. C. Penney's warehouse on Friday. On Saturday, the owner of a four-bedroom home at 9375 Gremlin Road, Stead, rented it at a reduced rate to Mrs. Bearer, her brother and his children. The phone and power companies are waiving utility installation charges.

Catherine Bearer said, "This is a town without strangers. We thank everyone."

An Easter Story

IT WAS so terribly wrong to murder the suspect. If only they had been guided by facts. He was innocent, but allegations were invented, the trial was a mockery to due process and then the lawless, emotional people killed the Man. Three days later, there occurred the Miracle of the Ages.

A story on this Easter Sunday.

It was the stormy, wintery night of February 19, his father's forty-eighth birthday, and twenty-year-old Thomas Cannon steered his pickup truck close to his parents' home on Foothill Road south of Reno's city limits. It was shortly before 7 o'clock. Soon he would be with his family at the birthday dinner for Dad.

He was virtually at Lois and Stephen Cannon's home when he remembered he had forgotten to get a birthday card. Tom Cannon turned the truck around. He would drive back to the Del Monte Shopping Center and buy a card. He was a happy, hardworking young man, a graduate of Wooster High School, who had gone for a year to Western Nevada Community College and was now employed at his father's tire company.

The rain persisted. Tom Cannon slowed, flicked on the left-hand turn signal, peered ahead for oncoming cars, made a final glance through his rearview mirror and began the turn left into the Del Monte Shopping Center. A driver of another northbound car had, an instant before, just missed hitting three pedestrians, a woman and two small girls.

The pedestrians were in young Cannon's path as he made his turn. He felt a bump and he knew he had hit something. He cleared the southbound lanes and rolled to a stop at the entrance of the darkened shopping center. He jumped from the truck, his heart pounding. He raced the few feet to the point of impact. It was 7:05 P.M.

He heard the cries of the injured mother, Catherine Bearer. Tom

218

Cannon picked up a dying little girl and carried her off the road and knelt with her, covering her with his coat.

Cannon ran to the phone booth outside Warehouse Market and called paramedics. Later, he called his father. "Dad, there has been an accident. A woman told me I have killed two people."

The dead were sisters Amy and Cathy Barr, ages eight and two.

Minutes afterward, Steve Cannon reached the accident scene and spoke to his son briefly, then watched as investigators snapped handcuffs on Tom and took him away. At a hospital, tests were given to determine the driver's blood alcohol level. At the sheriff's office, he was questioned and fingerprinted. An officer said to Tom Cannon, "I was once involved in a similar incident. I understand what you're going through." Tom Cannon was put in a cell. Though not charged, he was held three and a half hours pending investigation.

What has he been going through these ensuing forty-seven days? A living hell! He has been tormented by the enormity of the tragedy. In the first published account, the facts were confused. Investigators inadvertently made Tom Cannon's age twenty-eight instead of twenty. They had him driving south, instead of north, as was the case. There was the initial inference that Tom Cannon had too much to drink. In fact, he had had two beers and blood alcohol tests clearly show he was not intoxicated.

In these weeks of the young man's torment, sheriff's investigators, his attorney, W. H. Tobeler, and the legal staff of the Washoe County District Attorney's Office have painstakingly done their work. While Tom Cannon has languished in his valley of depression, the due process of our lawful society has been followed. Given the emotional aspects of the case, there existed in some citizens' minds a mental climate of "he's guilty." But there is a problem with jumping to conclusions before facts are determined.

Allegations can be invented in the mind's eye and often are. Public opinion based on hearsay can kill innocent men, and has.

The facts of this case are now determined. The Nevada Highway Patrol's detailed investigation has confirmed pedestrian error. Tom Cannon was not driving at a wrongful or illegal pace. The dead children, and their mother, were wearing dark clothing on that dark, wet night. Further, a storm the prior afternoon had knocked out of synchronization an automatic timing device that would have lighted the Del Monte Shopping Center's big lot as dusk came—and would have partially illuminated, too, the point of fatal impact. Instead, the lights did not turn on at the shopping center parking lot until 7:30 P.M., twenty-five minutes after the accident. There was no painted crosswalk at the site.

There have been a number of both injury and fatal accidents at the Del Monte entrance. The fact is that before the February 19 deaths of Amy and Cathy Barr, Warehouse Market owner Don Baldwin twice made urgent personal requests that the lethal site have a traffic light. No follow-up action had been taken.

On Good Friday just passed, nearly twenty centuries after the innocent Man received the ultimate punishment, Lois Cannon answered her telephone. She wept when she was told her son will not be charged. Due process is done. He is vindicated. Tom Cannon has a new life. He has new hope.

A Freakish Turning Point _____

IT WAS ONE of those freakish accidents that should never have occurred. Yet it did. A devilish turn in a great young life.

As with most accidents, it came without warning.

Brian Whalen had another great summer vacation stretching ahead, for he and his closest friends had just concluded their junior year at Reno High School. Three months away from the textbooks, then back to it. Brian hoped for an appointment to study at the U.S. Military Academy at West Point, where three generations of his mother's family had graduated, and where she had been born, the daughter of a career military officer.

He is a member of one of Reno's best-known families. Mother Kress Harris Whalen is a respected Alumni Council leader at the Nevada-Reno campus, active in many other organizations and stepdaughter of former Reno mayor Hugo Quilici. Brian Whalen, Sr., reared and educated in Boulder City, has a reputation that people admire: he is a former Nevada Engineer of the Year, a longtime member of the Washoe Regional Planning Commission and director of the Physical Plant, University of Nevada at Reno.

Yet, their son Brian needed no parental coattails, for he had established his own prominence.

Among the foremost Reno students academically, he has been student leader; hard worker; top athlete. If you took a vote among the soon-to-be Reno High seniors as to the most likely to succeed, Brian Whalen would be among the top finishers.

It was last Friday, June 12, late afternoon, the winding down of a hot day, and the young people, Brian included, were gathering for the swim party at the home of friends who live not far from the Whalen home in northwest Reno.

They rallied at poolside, sending up yelps of happy teenhood. There was no shoving or horseplay. Just a bunch of young adults gearing up for a happy time.

What a logical way to beat the heat. The treat of the cool water.

Brian was standing at the shallow end of the pool, at a depth of about three feet. He was about to take to the water, an entry that was to change his life.

Brian Whalen was an old pro around the water. A strong swimmer, he had for many months been churning up to 8,000 yards a day in practice sessions. One of the strongest competitors on the Reno High School swim varsity, he was a member of the Huskie relay team that captured a state championship just weeks ago.

As a seasoned water competitor, he had made the racing start dive into shallow water thousands of times.

But this time something went wrong.

Brian was not confused. He knew he was diving at the shallow not the deep end. He flattened out before hitting the water. But there was a miscalculation, a matter of only a degree or two, but enough to be critical.

Brian's friends heard a "different" sound as he hit the water, enough to alert them to trouble. His descent had been too steep and Brian's head had collided with the pool bottom, with little to cushion the impact. He had suffered wounds to his head that later required fourteen stitches. But the cuts were minor compared to the other wound.

Brian remembers what it was like before they reached him. He did not feel pain. He felt nothing. He lost his ability to move in those few seconds and he thought, "I can only hope they see me, because if they don't, I will drown."

Friends rushed to him.

Classmate Dirk Manoukian got to Brian first and three others followed and Brian remembers that his friend Jim Murphy shouted a warning as they eased him out of the water: "Hold his neck. Careful, hold his neck. Brian, don't move!"

Brian could not move. His neck was broken in two places. Paralysis came instantly.

In the St. Mary's Hospital room these past nine days, Brian Whalen has shown the thoroughbred qualities that run in champions. Though paralyzed from the neck down, only a few days later he was asking that the telephone be laid on his neck so he could talk to his friends and thank them for pulling him out. Two top neurosurgeons and an outstanding orthopedist are on his case and they are dealing with a patient who has courage and character, a seventeen-year-old who can pose the inevitable frank question that must be asked.

Stretched out in traction designed to ease his spinal column back into line, Brian Whalen speaks to the medical people: "What are my chances, doctor?"

"We are not optimistic that you will walk again, Brian."

In the first days following the accident, he had virtually no feeling. But in recent days, hopes have mounted that Brian will regain use of his arms and shoulders. There is slight feeling in his fingers. There is no movement from his chest down.

A renowned healer was in Reno this week. Catholic priest the Reverend Ralph DeOrio, of Massachusetts, whose presence earlier in the week in Las Vegas drew crowds of 9,000 on three straight nights, appeared two evenings at Little Flower Church.

On Wednesday night, he came to Brian Whalen's room at the hospital. A quiet, unpretentious man, the Reverend DeOrio prayed at Brian's bedside, asking that God help the good young man through this ordeal.

·§·§·§·§·

Brian Whalen, Jr., remains paralyzed. Nonetheless, he was graduated from the University of Nevada-Reno in 1987 with high distinction. An electrical engineering major, he contemplates studying for an advanced degree.

Anita's Caring Heart _____

HER NAME WAS Anita Marquart and she lived alone in a mobile home on a third of an acre she had bought in Sun Valley.

She had been an educator in the state of Washington and was supervisor of home economics at Washington State College until she reached retirement age. Miss Marquart never married and, with no one to look after her, she was especially frugal. She sewed all her own clothes and tucked away money in her savings, "for rainy days" and for use in the event she'd "need extras in her old age."

Miss Marquart moved to Reno to live out her retirement and it was natural for her to seek out companions of her age and persuasion.

She found them at Reno's Senior Center and in the Elderport program. She relied on the latter a lot for her transportation, as her own driving grew erratic with age.

She was an activist, a "fighter with style and class," remembers Elderport director Dorothy Pharis. "Anita empathized with society's have-nots. The elderly had a friend in her."

Senior Center director Judy Murphy recalls, "She was active in many community projects and was among those who pushed for constructing the Center, which finally was built in 1977–78."

She could be feisty. The turtle-slow bureaucracy especially rankled her, for she was by nature impatient with delay. The blizzard of paperwork was a special torment. "Why," she complained to friends, "must people take a year to do what we could do in a day?"

Miss Marquart wrote letters to the editor, urging local government to get off its hunkers. Her background in home economics fitted her beautifully to push successfully for a nutrition program for Sun Valley senior residents.

Her tall, slender, well-tailored figure was seen often around the Senior Center, where she was invariably engaged in animated conversation with friends.

She had the curiosity of a child, always probing to learn why things worked, or didn't. Anita Marquart developed an appetite for knowing about Elderport. Her questions brought insight. Elderport, she learned, is a fleet of thirty vehicles, a program to transport 3,000 meals a month to homebound elderly; Elderport is manned substantially by volunteers; it exists, she was told, to help wheelchair-bound people, young and old, to go see doctors, or go to shop.

Elderport, she soon knew, helps ferry handicapped people to workshops; all in all, it accrues some 8,500 one-way trips monthly, covering nearly 400,000 miles a year in Washoe County; approximately 4,500 people are directly served by the agency.

A year before her death last December of a malignant brain tumor at the age of seventy-eight, she was visiting the Elderport office. Almost as an aside, she said to director Pharis: "I hope I can leave something for Elderport. Maybe you could use it on transportation needs."

She delivered the comment in a low-key way. Yet, she was the kind who, we now know, truly meant it when she said, "I'll remember you in my will."

In developing her last will and testament, she gave specific instructions to her attorney, Robert C. Manley, and her wishes were carried out.

Upon her death, her friends learned how much she cared about them.

One of her most treasured possessions, her sewing machine, was left to the arts and crafts class at the Senior Center.

A total of $70,000, the bulk of her estate, was left to Elderport.

Elderport's directors have subsequently designated $10,800 of that sum to go to Reno's Senior Center. The money is being used to recarpet the center, which is visited by about 500 people daily.

As to the balance of the inheritance—Elderport has desperately needed its own maintenance site to keep those thirty vehicles operating efficiently and safely. "We're not transporting bread or milk," says Dorothy Pharis. "We move people—we need our motors and wheels in the best shape possible."

Elderport, thus, is negotiating to buy from Texaco, Inc., a former service station site at 1499 Wells Avenue, west of the Washoe County Fairgrounds. The price would be $85,000.

Anita Marquart's gift—and pennies and dollars donated by the elderly, plus an unsolicited personal $9,000 interest-free loan from a top Reno executive—has Elderport just about at its monetary goal.

"Every dime of the total," says Elderport's Pharis, "is private money, from people who care."

None cared more than Anita Marquart, who that day casually mentioned that she'd remember them in her will.

Requests for Christmas _____

ONE NIGHT last week, about twenty members of the Soroptimist Clubs of the area came to the Reno Senior Center to deliver Christmas cheer to the elderly.

As the veteran director of the senior citizen center, Judy Murphy, and her staff looked on, the Soroptimists helped decorate a large Christmas tree. They came bearing gifts—a 25-inch television set and reclining chair, among them. Soroptimists earlier had asked Lifetouch Portrait Studios to take pictures of the senior citizens and Lifetouch had done so—free of charge. At picture-taking sessions, some of the elderly had protested, "Oh, I'm too ugly," or "I'm too old." But the other night, those portraits were given to scores of people. Many wept when they saw the photographs. The comment "My family will love this" was heard again and again. Some seniors said they hadn't had their pictures taken in more than twenty years.

There were 160 persons who were not at the party. They are the Reno-area homebound, averaging seventy-five years of age.

Not long ago, Steve Freybarger and Jean Carr, representing employees of First Interstate Bank of Nevada, contacted Murphy. They said, "The FIB staff would like to do something special for senior citizens. We will erect a Christmas Wish Tree in our headquarters' lobby at 1 E. First Street, hang the seniors' wishes on the tree and fill those wishes."

Judy Murphy knew instantly that the perfect recipients of this generosity would be the homebound. In her mind's eye, she saw them out there in their little homes, thought of their frailties—many are bedridden; some have had strokes; there are those who have arthritis; those who have terminal cancer; those who suffer from Parkinson's disease.

Judy Murphy remembered that several use walkers or wheelchairs. A number are blind. They are predominantly widows and widowers. They are incapable of making the trip to the Senior Center or almost any other place—except maybe to the doctor's office. These 160 homebound have meager incomes—some less than $300 a month. The youngest of them is sixty, the eldest eighty-seven.

Murphy and her staff devised a questionnaire as a first step in fulfilling FIB's plan for a Christmas gift tree. The questionnaire was sent to the homebound. It asked them to check whether they would like such things as gloves, nightgowns, pajamas, shirts, blouses, slippers or food. Staff members Dorothy Keele and Roni Spoon added a final question: "Anything else you want or need?"

The returns were close to one hundred percent. Murphy was deeply touched by requests placed in that "anything else" category. "I tried to read them to the Soroptimist ladies the other night, but I choked up," Murphy said.

Murphy shared the replies with me; as I looked them over, I saw that their handwriting was shaky. Invariably, the messages came from people who live alone. The higher percentage of respondents were women. I share with you what some wrote in the "anything else" area.

"I'd like a tube of Ben-Gay and some knee socks," wrote Ava.

"May I have a bottle of rubbing alcohol?" requested Charlotte.

"If you want to give me a glass of jam or a package of cookies, I will thank Santa," wrote Edith.

"May I please have a Christmas corsage to wear on my coat when I go to church?" said Alice.

"Nothing I need right now. Thank you anyway," said Jack.

"I could sure use some wood for my fireplace," declared William.

"Please give me some boxer shorts, size 31; also white socks, regular size," requested Floyd.

"Is there a chance to get a robe?" asked Mildred.

"I'd love some peanut butter and crackers," confessed Orval.

"Snow boots, size $9\frac{1}{2}$ or 10," asked Louie.

Virtually everyone checked one category: food.

Raymond, who lives on B Street in Sparks, wrote one word in the space after "Anything else you need?" His request: "Friends!"

He added a postscript: "Thank you. There are others who need more."

Helping Mary Jane _____

LATELY, you have read in this space about that plucky young Carson City woman Mary Jane Buttner, and how she's fought, begged and pleaded for help. Has she needed help? You better believe it! A pocketful of miracles would fit her needs nicely, for she was born with a congenitally defective heart.

This condition can be corrected surgically. But the rub is cost. Mary Jane is an adult now, no longer eligible for Easter Seal Society funding help. For two years, she wrote or called politicians and bureaucrats. "Can't someone help me get this heart repaired before it's too late?" she cried. She pounded the pavement, asking assorted agencies for backing. What it came down to was everyone replying politely, but in the negative, "Sorry. But we have our rules." Doctors say she needs surgery within two months.

The chief problem is this—the Buttner parents reared six kids, two still at home. Father Jack Buttner had to take a disability retirement from Nevada Bell, after several back surgeries failed to mend him. Mary Jane Buttner, graduate of Carson High School, took a few courses at Western Nevada Community College. She manages full shifts as a bookkeeper. The family pays its bills but is not on Easy Street, by any stretch. Meanwhile, the young woman's energy has been flagging.

But you know, when you get down to the short strokes, whether it's in a voting booth or wherever people make important decisions, they have the wisdom and the heart to get worthwhile things done.

Mary Jane Buttner's story was first taken to the people who read this column. The message was that we ought to get behind this person and help. Once the people found out, wonderful things began occurring.

Jim Elston of Reno, a senior officer of First Interstate Bank, alerted FIB's East Carson branch office and a trust account has been established there. Gifts to the Mary Jane Buttner Heart Fund started coming and have grown. A Carson man gave $1,000; radio station KPTL told her story; Carson convenience stores used posters telling of her needs. From Greater Reno and from rural communities came pledges of help.

Women in Mason Valley called—they're going to hold a bake sale to benefit Miss Buttner. In came the gifts—such as $40 from Fallon's Ethel Ferguson and her son Bud—to name two benefactors.

The High Sierra Chefs' Association, comprised of 130 chefs, purveyors, food and beverage workers and salespeople, made a $500 commitment; employees of Nevada Bell, chiefly those based in Reno, contributed $700.

The largest corporate gift is a real beauty. Circus Circus is becoming more and more involved in significant charitable efforts, the most publicized case being that of cheerleader Valeria Pida, nineteen, from the University of Nevada-Las Vegas, who suffers from a form of cancer.

Circus Circus's entry into Mary Jane Buttner's case began a week ago when corporate officer Mel Larsen called me from Las Vegas. A few days later, Circus Circus's Reno marketing director Darlene Stout and vice-president Alvin Hummel confirmed a $5,000 contribution. Said Stout: "Circus Circus has been fortunate in its success, and wants to share that success with the less fortunate."

Meanwhile, Miss Buttner is trying to find a hospital and surgeon. Her cardiologist, Reno's Dr. Jerry Zebrack, says, "Her condition is deteriorating and the operation can't be put off much longer." But now comes the break she has been praying for.

Her predicament came to the attention of Dr. Robert Basta, general practitioner in Carson City and member of a longtime Nevada family. Basta, premedicine graduate of the University of Nevada-Reno, went to medical school at the University of Oregon in Eugene.

He has put Miss Buttner in touch with his Oregon classmate, surgeon Storm Floten, who has agreed to perform the surgery. It is to be done at St. Vincent Hospital, Portland, Oregon, one of the finest medical facilities in the Pacific Northwest. She will be admitted May 6; surgery is scheduled two days later.

The sum pledged for her now stands at about $7,500. It was initially estimated that $35,000 or more would be needed. But the goal has fallen to something closer to $15,000 because of the generous fee schedule pledged by St. Vincent Hospital and Dr. Floten.

·§·§·§·§·

A total of $24,000 was raised by Nevadans and Mary Jane Buttner subsequently had successful heart surgery in Portland.

Only Love to Give _____

FOUR YEARS AGO in Reno, transit bus driver Charles Long cheerfully welcomed a new passenger aboard. She was cordial and handsome Martha Truman, who had moved up here from Texas to teach school.

Long was single and it wasn't long before he learned she had never married. She became a regular rider on Long's route and formality disappeared; he became Chuck and she was Martha. They began dating and their affection and respect for each other deepened and they spoke casually of marriage. But there was plenty of time. They would wait awhile.

He was from a family of eight children, the leader his brothers and sisters invariably turned to.

But last Christmas he fell ill. He was extremely tired and had chills and fever. Frightened, he went for a physical. The verdict was bad. Charles Long, fifty-six, had cancer. Surgery was done and radiation treatment begun, but the malignancy had spread.

For most of the ensuing months, Long has stayed at the Riverside Convalescent Hospital on Idlewild Drive, where his family and Martha Truman, fifty-one, have rallied to him. The cancer has not been arrested, his decline continues, and his time grows short.

He has no material assets, no estate to leave. The medical bills are paid by government benefits and the State of Nevada. The only thing Charles Long has to offer Martha is love.

As his condition worsened, they talked anew of marriage. "Yes," she said, she would become his wife.

The time was set. The marriage would be at Riverside Hospital, the first ever performed there. And so last Friday at 6 o'clock in the evening, I joined thirty-seven persons including the couple's families, their closest friends and people on the Riverside staff. It was a beautiful ceremony, the most touching most of us will ever witness.

He was in his wheelchair in the facility's reception room, gaunt, his weight having shrunk to 118 pounds. Martha came to him on the arm of their best man. She stood with her man and took his hand. Flowers surrounded them. The champagne was chilled in the back of the room.

To their right, Ruth Sullivan, eighty-two, played the organ beautifully. Charles Long's physical therapist, Ronald Reed, twenty-two, sang "Getting to Know You."

St. Luke's Lutheran Church pastor John Handrich married them.

Charles Long's voice broke at first and Martha steadied him with her hand and a soft word.

They said to each other that they loved one another, that they will share all that is to come. They promised faithfulness and respect for each other and said they would work to keep their love and their marriage alive.

They said as God gives them life together, they intend to share as one life's challenges, joys and sorrows, victories and defeats.

As they spoke, each's voice grew stronger and we could see that the tears they had were happy ones. The Reverend Mr. Handrich stepped away and Martha and Charles Long kissed and clung to each other and cried.

Later, they opened their gifts, ate the cakes that had been given them, sipped the champagne and received the hugs and kisses of well-wishers.

A brother, William Long, of Elko, said he had never seen Charles as happy.

Martha Truman Long, a handsome bride, said, "I've told Chuck the only thing we can do is take each day at a time. We are in God's hands. Lord knows, He's the only one who can help us. If He doesn't help us, I don't know where we'll be."

After everyone had left, Martha and Charles were driven to a hotel to stay overnight. He returned to the Riverside Hospital the next day, and Martha went again to her trailer home.

As his treatments continue, she is with her man throughout the day. That is the way it is when the only thing you have to give is love.

A Rescued Life _____

SOME YEARS AGO, a Reno man had been living recklessly, imperiling himself by a drinking habit that had gone from casual to torrential. He became prey to alcohol, which has a stealthy way of bushwhacking its victims. Those who knew him say he likely would have died long ago if he hadn't been rescued by his involvement in Alcoholics Anonymous.

He did die a few days ago, of natural causes. When his AA friends were told of his death not long before Thanksgiving Day, they gave thanks that they knew him; they cried for him; all agreed he was "always there when somebody needed him." Someone remembered that just a few days after he suffered a stroke two months ago, he was out helping talk an alcoholic out of one more drink.

The miracle that AA offers, staying sober one day at a time, had rubbed off on this man. His story is both inspirational and instructive.

Suffice to say that his pre-AA days were difficult and that he was a potential human wreck. What happened to him subsequently is what matters most, because he was to live out his life in a way that we can learn by.

He worked at being kind, helpful and reliable; once pushy, he became cooperative; his loving and considerate nature, long obscured by drinking, resurfaced; he didn't look back on wasted times, but dwelled on present treasures; he gave helpful advice, but he didn't force-feed his opinions; it was said of him that he spoke the language of the loving heart.

He must have been a man who deserved credit for angry words no longer spoken, for temptations scorned, for his numerous good deeds, which he did not advertise.

From his adversity rose an awareness of what a good life is all about. At this time, let us relate ourselves to such a good life. Let us give our thanks for our own day-to-day treasures, so commonplace that we do not always see and savor their details.

Thanks for our part of the world, with its immense possibilities for our personal enjoyment, a place awash with beauty, heavy with delights and laden with scenes that gratify us—gorgeous sunsets, the glow of moonlight, the magical seasonal wonders; the serenity of our parks, the majesty of our mountains, lakes and streams; let us marvel at the music that increasingly surrounds us, and at the creativity of our artists; thanks for the growing concern our people have that our water, our air, our space, be fit as a fiddle.

Thanks for the innocence of our young and the wisdom of our elderly, and may their strengths nudge us with more than a glancing blow; thanks for making us remember that our best adult work can be the scaffolding that holds up our lives; we rejoice anew in daily miracles—clothing, a roof, heat, remembered conversations with teachers, friends, family and some who have no more tomorrows.

We can profit in the discovery made by our aforementioned late friend—let us not botch the job of making friends, of helping neighbors; let us give a wide berth to the disease called boredom; live not in unhealthy competition, but in joyous cooperation.

In the Talmud, that collected body of Jewish wisdom, it is written, "In the world to come, each of us will be called to account for all the good things God put on the earth, which we refused to enjoy."

Every new friend we meet, each new truth unearthed, every fresh experience, can make us richer. Wrote Harold Kushner, in his wonderful book *When All You've Ever Wanted Isn't Enough*: "Life is a work of art, and if we have taken loving attention to the details, we'll be pleased with the finished product."

And we speak of the religions of man—from mud huts in Africa and igloos in Labrador to the Yemenite Jews in their synagogues in Jerusalem; to Istanbul, as they prostrate themselves toward Mecca; to a swami who lives at the foot of the Himalayas; to monks in Kyoto and people in the privacy of the Buddhist shrine; to ourselves—there is a divine architect of what we are and what we have; call the Master what you wish, Holy Author or God.

He made life, and it is no meaningless accident; may we please agree that God doesn't believe we'll live our lives with a perfect score, but that we at least ought to earn a passing grade! That a meaningful life is seldom achieved by a few great immortal deeds, but is chock-full of a lot of little ones! We do pass through life a bit like authors and actors, and we should perform our roles as best we can.

We think of the wisdom of the six words author Kushner wrote, "We should go about doing good." It is difficult to imagine a superior objective.

STRICTLY
PERSONAL

The Story of Mel _____

IT WAS A YEAR AGO today that the call came reporting that the man they called Mel had died.

He had reached the age of sixty-nine, which was incredible in itself, for he long had suffered from diabetes and emphysema and all their miserable related effects. So now it was over and Mel's small family and his friends agreed it was better this way.

I flew to Boise, Idaho, for the funeral. His wife had asked me to do the eulogy and when I arrived, she showed me the obituary in the *Idaho Statesman*. It was ever so brief and unemotional, as such stories are, and I knew these facts of Mel's life so very well, and know so much more.

I delivered the eulogy to Mel to the not more than twenty-five people who attended and I thought, "God, is this all there is?" So few there to say good-bye. Yet, it made sense: Mel had been a baker all his working life and he lived in the obscurity of the nonpublic class; despite the illnesses that long hounded him, he'd outlived many of his friends; many who were left were too frail to attend.

But to me, Mel was a hero who had achieved, against great odds, a goal he once thought impossible. If one vote counted, then mine puts him in any book on Profiles in Courage.

The eulogy offered the facts and I think most in the sparse audience were stunned, for few knew his story.

The facts were these:

His parents moved west to Boise from Kentucky after the turn of the century, and Mel was the youngest of six children. He was ignored by his alcoholic father and spoiled by his doting mother and by the time he was eighteen, he, too, was a slave to the bottle. He married at twenty-two, had a son and a daughter; in the grip of his master, alcohol, he beat his wife. The marriage ended in 1935. He went his sad way, in the grip of a habit much stronger than himself, bouncing from job to job, ignoring child support payments, finally failing at a second marriage and making the newspaper's "driving while intoxicated list" many times.

He was intelligent and tremendously humorous and, in his sober hours, contrite. But it was down, down, down for Mel. He drank away the best of intentions and inebriation seemed to be his life sentence. Those who knew him knew he'd forever be a prisoner.

But in 1952, when he was forty-three, he married for a third time, to an understanding, strong woman. She laid out the facts more bluntly than had those before: "Find a solution, or die while yet a young man."

That same year, he found the answer. Alcoholics Anonymous helped him see that there was a way. He heard the others tell of their personal miracles. He pulled himself away from the bottom. He visited Boise's skid row over and over, not as resident, but as rescuer of others. He was caught up in an evangelistic mood, selling AA to the people he'd once spent lost weekends with. And it worked. Now, for the first time, he amounted to something and he knew it.

Mel spent the rest of his life—twenty-six years—dry, staying sober one day at a time. In his turnaround, he was a dependable worker, a dedicated family man and, to those few who knew his story, a true hero.

The eulogy paid Mel tribute for the accomplishment, and for much more, and I said his family would not forget his great example, nor cease to admire it. Finally, I said I had respected and loved my father, Rollan Melton, Sr., so very much.

Annie _____

It is my moment of truth. True confession time.

There is a new love in my life.

It isn't all that often that a man feels compelled to tell all in public print. But a rather substantial number of people already know how I feel about her, so I might just as well tell all.

Who knows? Perhaps in time she will come to love me just as much as I love her, and love her I do, truly and surely.

This has all come over me so quickly, for it was but four days ago that I first met her.

But love is like that. That special feeling can require years, even decades to take hold. Or it can overpower one in the instant of first meeting.

With Annie, it happened in an instant.

Simply a first glimpse of Annie, the brown hair and blue eyes and that cute baby face, and I was smitten.

Is there a more powerful force than the compelling force of a handsome woman, even when she ignores you? I doubt it.

I had been awaiting her first visit for months and it had been indicated we would meet in late May. She would not be more precise as to time.

The telephone rang one recent morning.

"Your special friend is en route. Arrival time is to be in Reno, as planned, and within the next few hours. Sorry. But we can't be more specific. You know how these schedules are."

I went to the appointed place and waited and waited.

"Annie, hurry along now!"

Time moved on and there was some pacing and it was indicated that finally she had arrived.

"Just a few more minutes and Annie will see you."

All right.

241

Then we met. I swept sweet Annie into my arms, and I was ruled by my bias. She was beautiful.

She seemed so relaxed and, quite frankly, oblivious to me, but nevertheless I held her to me and kissed her cheek and I couldn't help it: I stared at her a lot.

Another man in her life, this one much more important, ordered, "Turn this way. That's it."

Annie squirmed. I turned her to the camera and I smiled and that first picture was taken, with many more to come.

Our son Wayne extended his hand and we had a joyous handshake and he said:

"Congratulations. Annie is twenty minutes old and she's your first grandchild and how do you like her so far?"

"That's easy, son. A new love in my life. Truly and surely."

The Curiosity of Grandchildren _____

IN MY TIME, and that's quite a long spell, kids, I've been questioned by the best inquirers. Cops have grilled me, and so have critics, newspaper colleagues, my one wife, only mother-in-law and a whole batch of other probers.

Last week, I met my match. I must admit the little Melton sisters, Annie and Bonnie Melton—my granddaughters, ages five and four—had all the best of me. I was on vacation all week, and my wife Marilyn and I baby-sat the children.

Now I am back at work, having fled happily to my office, to get a well-deserved rest. As I flail away at this writing machine, I reflect back on last week. It was such fun being with these little dandies—it was my friend Don Jessup who noted last year, "If I'd known grand-children were so much fun, I'd have had them first," and Don was so correct.

But the children's questions were too much for me. When one has been away from the little ones for a few years, one tends to forget the vast array of inquiry that vaults from such tender minds.

A sampling of questions I faced:

"Grandpa, why are you old?"

"Who is Marie Callender? Is she the cook? Why doesn't she come out of her kitchen? Did she help build this restaurant? Is Mrs. Callender married?"

"What is snow and why does it come down?"

"Grandpa, how long ago were you a little child?"

"Does Wilbur May live in this museum? How long did it take him to shoot all these animals? Why is the giraffe so tall? How tall is he? Why don't they take down that wall so we can see the bottom half of Mr. May's giraffe? How long did it take Mr. May to travel around the world more than forty times?"

"Grandpa, how do you spell arboretum?"

"How does the Dairy Queen make these hot dogs?"

"Grandpa, if milk shakes make people fat, why are you drinking yours?"

Grandpa Moses _____

THE FIRST TIME I saw my future father-in-law, he scared me half to death.

It was 1952. I had stopped at Dorothy and Bill Royle's Reno home for the first time, to collect their eighteen-year-old daughter Marilyn for our first date.

My future wife introduced me to her father and I could swear he was glaring at me. "Get her in early!" he shouted.

Naturally, he was showing real unease. I didn't understand then. Now, as a father of my own teenage daughter, I do.

It took me five years to stop calling him Mr. Royle. And sir.

I have known this incredible Nevadan for twenty-eight years and each day my respect for him increases. To me, Bill Royle is not only father-in-law deluxe, but Mr. Nevada as well.

He has many high points in his career as a public man—all of those years being in Nevada, where he moved in 1912 as a seventeen-year-old.

The first night I met him, I didn't possess a thimbleful of knowledge about his background. If I had, there would have been more tremble in me than there was—and downright awe.

Bill Royle had served in France during World War I, and by the time he was elected to the Nevada Assembly in 1921, he was but twenty-five years old—one of the youngest so elected.

Later, he was to start up the Social Security office in Reno, and he was among northern Nevada's first Internal Revenue agents.

One of the world's great wonders, Boulder Dam, was being constructed and they sent in none other than Bill Royle to keep the peace between management and labor. He was then the state's labor commissioner.

The man I was to become so intimately acquainted with was Nevada's manpower leader during World War II.

244

By the time I met him, he was running things at Social Security and shortly thereafter would become postal service leader in northern Nevada.

Bill Royle was born in Ogden, Utah, in 1895, one of twelve children born to an English couple who moved to the United States in 1885.

Many of his brothers and sisters were artistic, but Bill wasn't—or so everyone thought. He was a teenager working on the Northern Nevada Railroad out of Ely. Then a twenty-two-year-old doughboy in France. Then to the Nevada political scene. It was Royle who introduced the gas chamber penalty measure to the Nevada Legislature. He made an unsuccessful run for Nevada secretary of state in 1926.

Bill Royle finally hung it up as a Nevada public figure in 1959, retiring with thirty-eight years of government service.

For the last twenty-one years, he's been in low-profile retirement around Reno, where he and Dorothy have lived since 1935.

But around the house, we've enjoyed that marvelous voice, which ranges somewhere between a roar and a growl. My father-in-law has alternately been Mr. Fix-It, and the finest pal any ten grandkids could own.

Part curmudgeon, part marshmallow and all Republican, he has provided anyone within the range of his gravel-voice with as sound an education on state history and politics as one could get anyplace.

Like so many retirees, he has moved largely unheralded among the young. Obviously, at age eighty-five, he is older than almost everybody else, having outlived long-ago friends. He is now surrounded by younger people who somehow believe it is they who have lived in the most troubled and perilous of times.

But like so many other seniors, Bill Royle not only won his spurs, he keeps inventing new ones.

Now he has become a successful artist. The boy nobody thought had a lick of artistic ability has again proven himself special.

The art focus developed late in his eighty-fourth year. Daughter Marilyn bought him paints, brushes and an easel. He was off and running, producing his first work in February 1979. Bill Royle has since done nearly fifty pieces, most of them oils. During all of December, he is featured in a one-man art show at the Reno Senior Center.

I look at his work as objectively as I can. And I think it's great. This is not a sunset, but a new career, a new dawn for still young Bill Royle, age eighty-five.

·§·§·§·§·

William Royle continued his art career to the end of his life, finishing his final oil a few days before his death on October 12, 1984, at the age of eighty-nine.

Say it Isn't So!

TODAY'S STORY began two months ago on a pleasant and sunny November day.

I drove west on Interstate 80 over the gorgeous Sierra, a happy guy, playing my music, having my cigarettes, not a concern to my name.

It was my usual physical examination run over to the Woodland Medical Clinic north of Sacramento. Ho hum. Routine. My ninth straight year. I thought ahead of what the doctor would say: "Lose some more weight. You really should try harder to quit smoking." I knew this script by heart. I knew I would nod agreement and later go back and work harder on weight control. But as to cigarettes— well, thought I, I'm only forty-nine and trouble only visits the other guy.

Dr. John Hermanovich, internist, gave me the predictable weight and smoking lecture and said they would give me the results when available. I drove home a happy man.

The following Monday, November 24, Dr. Hermanovich called me at my office at 1:31 P.M. He said: "Your chest X ray was not normal. There is a suspicious area on the upper middle of your left lung. It could be an infection, or a cyst or a tumor."

The doctor talked and I reached for a cigarette, then jerked my hand away.

"The thing that concerns me," Dr. Hermanovich said, "is that your chest X ray just one year ago was normal. The suspicious area ought to be evaluated without delay."

Stunned, I mumbled agreement. I was to revisit Woodland Clinic to see a pulmonary specialist. This time, it wouldn't be a routine encounter.

Dr. Louise Wong hit me with questions and I squirmed. Most seemed to concern my history as a heavy smoker. Yes, I was a three-pack-a-day man. Yes, I had smoked for many years.

She immediately probed, "How many years?"

"Since I was twenty-three. Total of twenty-six years."

An hour later, I was next door in Woodland Memorial Hospital as an outpatient. Dr. Wong had inserted an instrument through my nostril, thence through my throat and into my lung area. She could see inside me and she was trying to get right on top of the suspect area, to obtain tissue samples for biopsy. The suspect spot was tucked away from the airway and was tough to get to. But she came close. She said, "We will evaluate and call you after the laboratory does its work."

I drove home with my thoughts and a clean ashtray. Frightened, I had quit cold. How damned foolish to have disregarded for all these years the Blue Ribbon Panel findings, the doctors' cautions, the pleas of family and friends.

Cursed tobacco habit! Cancer fear gnawed at me.

If only my doctors would now agree with my unspoken plea, "Say it isn't so."

The weekend passed. Dr. Wong called me in Reno. "Although we cannot find cancer cells, we suggest you return again for additional consultation and tests."

So, I was at Woodland again and visiting with still another doctor. I had kept the situation pretty quiet back in Nevada. The *Reno Gazette-Journal* kept saying, "Melton is on special assignment."

Woodland surgeon Dr. Dean Winn wasn't about to say, "It isn't so." He said: "Although we cannot find cancer cells, your X ray is highly suspicious. The spot is a bit more than an inch in diameter and it is configured as a tumor often is. There was nothing there prior to your 1979 X ray. Foremost, there is your history of heavy smoking. Mr. Melton, I believe you most likely have a malignant tumor in the lung. It should be removed. I would suggest you not wait long to make a decision."

I didn't want Dr. Winn to say all this. Why couldn't he say, "Everything is going to be all right. It's all been a mistake"?

I asked more questions. I tried to structure them so he would offer me hope. The surgeon just kept coming back with more facts.

We settled on 9:30 A.M., December 18, for my lung surgery.

I was admitted to Woodland Hospital on December 17. The next morning, surgeon Winn, if he found cancer, would take some of the lung, all of it, or "close me up and send me home." But first, they took a new chest X ray and made a new blood test—all nearly a month after the initial findings.

"Something's unusual here," Dr. Winn told me. "The lung spot has reduced in size." It was perhaps twenty-five percent smaller. I could barely believe it. Prayers answered? Yes. New tests, including a needle biopsy deep into the chest, were done. Still no cancer cells. Surgery was canceled.

"Go home," said Dr. Winn, "and return January 15 for a new X ray."

Last Thursday, at Woodland, they took a new picture. The suspect area had again decreased in size. Dr. Winn looked at me, now a confirmed nonsmoker, and he said, "It looks like what you have is a nonmalignant, chronic inflammation, or infection."

I told him I had not smoked in seven weeks. "Has that helped make this thing shrink?" Surgeon Winn has a classic way of understating facts. He looked at me and nodded and said, "It is likely that cessation has helped a great deal."

So I am home again, happy again. It wasn't cancer. I am one of the lucky ones.

The Lethal Habit _____

LAST SUMMER, as my sister lay dying, we had the frankest talks we'd ever had with each other. We had laughed together, until near the end when her emphysema made it so difficult for her and then we cried together.

Days before the illness took her, she asked me if I would someday write for the people, telling them how foolish she had been to have been a smoker. "But wait until I'm gone," she ordered. "I hope what you say will scare hell out of people."

Today, I share with you the story Bronna Melton Reynolds wanted you to hear. I selected this day because it is the ninth annual Great American Smokeout, that time when smokers are asked to give up tobacco for twenty-four hours. An estimated fifty-one million Americans still smoke; thirty-three million have quit smoking. My sister was one of them. But for her, it was too late. There has been on both sides of our family a genetic disposition to emphysema, that cruel disease that attacks the lungs, throttling them, robbing them of life-giving health.

To smoke on top of the genetic weakness was to fly in the face of good sense. Yet both of us had been smokers. Bronna lit up when she was still in high school. I was out of college by the time I got hooked. I am talking about the late 1940s and early 1950s, when smoking was cool, accepted, when you did it "because others did it." I quit smoking five years ago. Bronna also tried. Her cessation didn't come in time.

She was a lovely girl, handsome, with a rapier wit. We were the only kids in our family and we had been extremely close when we were young, but then, as happens too often, we drifted from each other to do our own thing. Bronna lived in other states and I traveled a lot in years past.

After her marriages came apart, she had to raise her two sons alone. Finally, she got back to Nevada, and I got off my administrative treadmill and returned to my typewriter, sticking in one place. I was still in Reno and Bronna was again back in our hometown, Fallon. The last seven years, we saw each other a lot, corresponded, and wore out the telephone.

Her health began to stagger in 1980. At first she couldn't figure what it was, this tiredness and shortness of breath. "Just getting old, Sunny boy," she joked with me. But God, she was then only forty-seven.

Then a parade of doctors confirmed the brutal truth. She had emphysema. "What you have can't be cured," each told her. "But if you quit smoking now, maybe we can get this progression stopped in its tracks."

Bronna cut back her cigarette consumption, but the few she smoked each day seemed as lethal as the packs a day she once smoked. In her last year and a half, she quit entirely. But fatal harm already had been done.

The damage of cigarette-fueled emphysema was an ugly sight. In the last two years, Bronna was entirely dependent on those portable oxygen tanks we brought in. Her personal travel was confined to the brief drive to Reno, where, at St. Mary's Hospital, she would undergo physical therapy. The treatment didn't help. A walk across her small living room became an agonizing marathon.

She was hurting so bad. The woman whose great personality had thrilled us all began to snap angrily at any smoker who came within a half-block of her. "Get away from me with your goddamn cigarettes!" My sister would pound her fists on her furniture and denounce herself. "Why was I so foolish to smoke?" She would say again and again, "Anybody who smokes is as great a fool as me."

Bronna had been a wonderful artist, but as her final spring arrived, she could not summon enough energy to drag herself to her drawing board. Her endless regimen of pills had become a way of life as her physicians tried to find comfort levels for her. In the night, the most frightening period of all, she would be seized by bronchial spasms and she would believe her time had come. Some people who become ill with emphysema have never smoked a cigarette. My sister was convinced that smoking was the only reason she fell ill.

Summer came and she knew more clearly than any of us that it would be her last. Bronna summoned a Methodist minister and he baptized her in her home in what she said was the great moment of her life.

I drove to visit her on July 5 and she was having a wretched day in a Fallon hospital. The next morning, we spoke by phone and she could barely summon the breath to say she loved me. Bronna died a few hours later.

My sister's death certificate lists the cause of her death: tobacco dependency.

A Story that Will Do Your Heart Good _____

Editor's Note: Rollan Melton's column resumes today after a sixteen-week disappearing act that began when he suffered a coronary. His topic today: You've Got to Have Heart.

NEXT TIME you are tempted to deceive yourself into believing it will never happen to you—"It's always the other guy"—remember these words, or at least my theme.

I thought it would be the other guy, too! So much for my carelessness, ignorance and myopic vision.

So, I write again for you today, setting down words about myself. Yet, I trust many of you will profit by relating them to yourselves and the people you care about.

The Nevada summer was heating up. As June wound down, so did I.

I had had a recurring signal in days leading up to June 26 that my body wasn't clicking on healthful cylinders. But I didn't recognize the signal, which was an on again/off again pain in the back of the neck. Even had I sensed danger, I probably would have ignored it, because "it always happens to the other guy."

As I look back, about the only thing I had done right for my health, in the many years leading up to my problem, was quitting cigarette smoking, cold-turkey, nearly two years ago. As Melton luck would have it, the cessation of tobacco probably saved my life.

Dawn was about to break on Saturday, June 26. I had had a restless night, for I had a pain in the neck, later diagnosed as angina.

I had slept little, so when 5:15 A.M. arrived, I got up. Hey, maybe this would be the day I'd crack a certain weight plateau, I thought. I had been on a weight-reduction kick of late, dieting and walking five slow-paced miles a day.

I toddled downstairs, feeling somewhat weary. I chalked up the fatigue to my restless night. I lumbered onto the scales, thus becoming one of the few people who ever weighed during a heart attack and lived to tell about it.

My upright medical scale shuddered under the load and the needle rested on 249.8 pounds. "Man, I've cracked 250!"

Some victory!

I started back up the stairs. Fatigue suddenly closed in like a ton of Fallon hay atop me. I hauled myself up slowly.

I limped into the bathroom. A numbness now assailed my left arm. I broke into a sweat, drenching the nightclothes within seconds.

I looked in the mirror. I saw the chalky face of a man in deep trouble.

My wife Marilyn summoned our physician and close friend Noah Smernoff, who lives nearby. He had his stethoscope pressed to my clammy chest within ten minutes. No more than eight or nine more minutes elapsed before three Medic-I men came to my bedside. They had that "you are going with us" look, and I was eager to obey, for Dr. Smernoff had told me seconds before, "This looks like a coronary, all right."

Two of them eased me onto a stretcher. Small men with big, strong hands. As they carried me down our back steps and out into the spreading Reno dawn, I figured if the heart attack didn't kill me, they'd drop my over-fed body and I'd die in the fall.

Emergency at St. Mary's Hospital was geared for my arrival. So was a man I'd never met, but have since come to admire greatly. Cardiologist Stanley Thompson moved in swiftly and had an electrocardiogram reading on me within a few minutes. He leaned down to whisper the most reassuring words I have ever heard: "You are having a heart attack, but if you must have one, this is the best kind to have."

On what I since named the Cardiac Richter Scale of 10, I was hit with about a 4.

Those critical first seventy-two hours passed without another "hit." I was buried under a mass of wires, tubes and the loving and professional care of St. Mary's Cardiac Care Unit people. I remember looking at all that gear, having been stabilized by the great medicines and the wonderful people, knowledge and equipment, and thinking, "Science and mankind's heart and resolve have made this all possible. The next time somebody criticizes research, I think I'll punch him out."

An effective way to become a cripple is to lie in bed and wither. They had me up and walking as the third day ended. On the tenth and final hospital day, cardiologist Thompson had me on a treadmill, doing up to two miles an hour.

I returned to St. Mary's Hospital less than two weeks later for an important test. In the hospital's super-modern angiogram facility, X rays were taken of my heart. The coronary had indeed wiped out one of the major arteries. Once a part of your heart dies, the tissue is dead forever. The good news, however, is that of the two remaining arteries, one has only twenty to twenty-five percent plaque (arteriosclerosis), while the other is free of heart disease. "This means," my cardiologist friend reassured me, "that no coronary bypass surgery is needed at this time."

It's up to me to do all in my power to arrest my heart disease.

This goal, stay as healthy as I can become, can only be achieved by forever abandoning the life-style that made me "one of those other guys." I am advised that had I not ceased smoking three packs a day, I probably would have suffered a heart attack sooner, certainly a massive hit, and perhaps a fatal one.

One's healthy heart is apt to turn sour, as with my once healthy heart, with years of abuse.

I was overweight and didn't do anything about it. I gobbled artery-clogging dairy products: ice cream, whole milk, cheese, eggs; I ate too many fatty foods; my work hours were too long; it was easier for me to join this organization, or that, instead of declining.

Unfortunately, sometimes I have to get hit in the head by an anvil to get the message. Or hit in the heart.

But now I know, as well as any person can know, the error of my past ways. In my quest to live with as healthy a heart as diet and exercise can produce, I've launched into a new life-style.

Spurred by new knowledge, buoyed by a return to what feels to me to be top physical shape, I have turned 180 degrees from that pre-June life.

Living with a new eating way of life, my weight is now 194 pounds, down from 250; I'm not flying helter-skelter across the country; I've found the magic of a reasonable work and play schedule; no more cranking out columns at the rooster's first crow. A 9 A.M. starting time is good enough for me.

The guy who formerly shunned brisk exercise like the plague is now walking several miles daily. The guy who used to crack such self-deprecating jokes as "I have a glandular problem; each gland weighs 100 pounds"—that guy will have to find new jokes.

I'm not yet exactly the epitome of "Fat to Fit" that my dear, dear St. Mary's Hospital friends urged me to become.

But there's one thing they and so many others have sold me on.

You've got to have heart. A healthy one. An optimistic one.

Not His Best Day

THIS ISN'T false modesty. The fact is, a couple of weeks ago, Ron Watson called me, made me chuckle with a couple of his patented one-liners, then sprang a huge surprise. The executive director of the Greater Reno–Sparks Chamber of Commerce was a beaming messenger.

Watson told me the Chamber was naming me recipient of its Civic Leader of the Year award. The reasons continue to elude me, but my deep pleasure is rooted to stay. Suffice to say I am delighted at the Chamber's lack of thorough checking.

One of my virtues must have caught the selectors' eyes. I pride myself on being prompt, on making meetings on time, and I say further that those who cut into my time with their tardiness drive me bananas. Up the wall. Make me chew at my guts. Cause my blood pressure to soar.

One other nice thing. I am a conservative drinker. I've seen alcohol mess up too many lives. I never want mine to be one of them. But now to the point of this story.

If the Chamber, in its wisdom, could have watched me scramble ingloriously last Thursday, it would have rescinded its decision.

Last Wednesday night, I went alone to the dress rehearsal of *Sheep Dip 1986* and laughed hard, drank white wine, watched the late-night critique of the rehearsal and drank more white wine. Then I joined friends Ruth and Stan Brown and Arthur Johnson at the Hilton Hotel bar downstairs. I drank more white wine. I sure hope the three are still my friends. I haven't heard from them since.

The Browns accompanied me home, a bit of wisdom they insisted upon. A personal note now. I awake like clockwork at 5 in the morning and I don't need an alarm. For years, I've caught 6:45 A.M. jets out of Reno with nary a nudge from the wife, or a wake-up call. Nothing. Also, I am not aware that I have walked in my sleep since my early adult years.

The Browns must have gotten me home about 1:15 A.M. Thursday. Marilyn stirred her sleepy head. "You OK?" I am now told I replied, "Yes."

At around 4 o'clock, she tells me, I got up and strode blindly into our walk-in closet. When Marilyn asked what I was doing, I am advised that I replied, "Looking for the numbers."

Later, the telephone rang a foot and a half from my left ear. I slept on. Another ring and then a third. An elbow clanked against my ribs. "Answer it!" my wife groaned.

I picked up the receiver and my secretary, Mickey Wessel, said, "Your out-of-state visitor is waiting for you. Aren't you coming in?"

"Who's waiting?" I screeched.

"Mr. Ward."

I said, "Good God, what time is it?" and Mickey answered, "It's 8:26."

"Jeeze, Louise, stall him, Mickey. Keep him talking. I'm on my way."

I shaved in two minutes, cleverly letting the straight razor whack off a slice of chin. When I fled the house at around 8:35, I was a total mess. Blood on my chinny-chin-chin and appearing for all the world like I'd been dropped into my suit from high altitude.

My mind raced ahead. After Mr. Ward (I'd never met him before), I had that speech with Warren Lerude's journalism class at the university at 10. God almighty, I hadn't done that speech outline yet.

Ward was a true sport. Even as he gazed at my unshowered body and bloody chin, he smiled and pretended that this behavior is commonplace. As we chatted, I firmed a timetable in my head. I have preached promptness to onetime newspaper colleague Lerude for years. I couldn't be a second late arriving at the campus.

Ward screwed up my plan. "Can you drop me off uptown? I am walking and besides, I broke my toe not long ago."

Damn, damn. How do you say no to a virtual cripple? I raced him uptown, abruptly dumped him and saw by my watch that the detour had cost me at least five minutes. When I reached the campus, I lost another three minutes finding parking.

I tried to sprint toward the building and saw two startled coeds. No doubt it was the first look they've had of a hydrant-shaped man, clad in a rumpled suit and holding Kleenex to his chin.

I ran into Lerude's class at an embarrassingly tardy 10:04. He was pacing nervously and his bright class was there, staring with impatient wonder at the visiting expert.

Lerude let me use the outline of the same speech I'd made for his students in 1985. The kids pummeled me with questions. Afterward, Lerude lied to me for the first time in all these years. He told me I did good. My topic for his class: management efficiency—timeliness.

Later, my wife locked herself out of our house and I had to rescue her. At 2 P.M. Thursday, I went to UNR for a meeting that was scheduled for twenty-four hours later. The same night, I misintroduced Rabbi Abraham Feinberg as "Weinberg."

Otherwise, I always will remember Thursday as a rather ordinary day.

Loving Each Newspaper Day _____

FORTY YEARS AGO this month, a weekly newspaper in Fallon, the *Standard*, hired me to be its teenage printer. I worked part-time, for about $10 a week, sweeping up the little shop, running errands and doing everything that everyone else avoided like the plague. I was fifteen.

At first, all I intended was to pick up pin money, then drift away. But a wonderful thing happened before I could skip to another temporary job.

Suddenly, I was meeting the most fascinating people! It was routine, for instance, for the famous Pat McCarran to drop by our office. More exciting were the Fallon townspeople, truly a collection of memorable citizens.

I was given the most formidable challenges a boy could imagine. I was urged to write for the public print: my bosses taught me to interview, to compose news stories, to work a typewriter: when I jabbered during interviews, they told me to shut up and listen.

A stupendous world opened up because of my entry into journalism. All at once, the boy who had earlier dropped out of high school was getting his diploma, and a scholarship to college. At the University of Nevada-Reno, where I studied journalism, I couldn't get enough of newspapering. I was incurably smitten. Journalism became my scholarship to life.

In those years, and every day since, an incredible parade of characters has visited my life, all because of the profession I stumbled into by accident. To this day—and it will be like this to the end—I see everybody as a potential story.

In these magical four decades, I have dealt with the wacky and the wonderful, the penniless and the millionaires, the babes and the boobs, the workers and the captains of industry. There have been rogues, heroes, achievers, villains.

In Nevada, and across the country, my calling has given me a front-row seat to life. As Shakespeare wrote, life is a stage and all the men and women merely players.

What I've seen is no dress rehearsal. It's real.

What a treat to have watched the changing cast of players and, for some of the years, to have overseen newspapers that filed the daily news reports about their communities.

In the beginning, I was boy printer, then cub reporter. After my army public information years, I became a sports editor in Reno, dreaming then of becoming a famous sports columnist. Oh, to be the contemporary Red Smith! But fate got in the way. I didn't realize when they dragged me kicking and screaming to my first management job that one of the largest adventures was just ahead.

They made me an editor. When I failed to mismanage that task fully, I became publisher. Then it was on to the presidency of Speidel Newspapers, Inc., a nationwide media company based in Reno. All of a sudden, as rookie president, I was leading Speidel into becoming a publicly owned company. All this made me curse myself for having steered completely clear of anything resembling a business course at UNR.

In those ensuing years, I collided with a business world I could not envision in my growing-up years: the world of Wall Street, price earnings, takeover threats, the day's closing stock quotes. My world wasn't news sources and fellow reporters anymore, but lawyers, accountants; securities analysts.

Ten years ago, on May 11, 1977, the Speidel firm, smallest of the public newspaper companies, merged its thirteen dailies with the premier media company, Gannett, a move that has prospered readers of the former Speidel cities across the country. I stayed on as a senior vice-president of Gannett for a year and a half, even moving from Reno to New York state for a summer. But I had been telling my wife for years, "Someday, believe me, I've got to get back to my typewriter. Writing is what drew me to newspapering in the first place. I want to go back again, be with people, tell their stories."

Back to writing I came, eight and a half years ago, more than 1,500 columns ago. I have never been happier in my profession than in the years since October 1978. I talked to thousands of people, chronicled their ups and their downs, told of their humor and talked in general about life in this most pleasant part of our world. Mostly, the words have dwelled on a multitude of positives.

Nevadans have made this period my most delicious newspaper time. To all of you, I remain grateful.

It takes an incredible breadth of talent to produce good newspapers—advertising, business, production and circulation and distribution talent. But my heart belongs first in the newsroom. That's where the foremost joy has been for me for forty years.

And the joyous beat goes on.

Appendix ───────────────────────────

The pieces included in this volume originally appeared on the dates cited below in the *Reno Evening Gazette* (REG) and the *Reno Gazette-Journal* (RGJ).

Home Means Nevada

Nevada	*October 29, 1979*	**REG**
Summer	*June 22, 1980*	**REG**
Autumn	*September 9, 1979*	**REG**
I Do Love You	*February 14, 1979*	**REG**
Sweet Deeds	*March 19, 1980*	**REG**
50,000 Weddings	*January 9, 1983*	**RGJ**
An Evening in Wellington	*October 19, 1980*	**REG**
Rural Postal Team	*July 15, 1984*	**RGJ**
Wild Nicknames	*December 7, 1979*	**REG**
Italian Honor Roll	*August 3, 1986*	**RGJ**
Truckee Treasures	*October 27, 1978*	**REG**

Soldiers and Sailors

The Lasting Pain of War	*May 25, 1980*	**REG**
Fallon's War Heroes	*December 6, 1981*	**REG**
Once There Was a War	*April 22, 1979*	**REG**
Purple Heart Kid	*September 23, 1979*	**REG**

Tales People Have Told Me

The Picture of Will Rogers	*March 16, 1986*	**RGJ**
Pearl's Friends	*March 16, 1979*	**REG**
Broke on a Lonely Road	*November 29, 1981*	**REG**
Christmas Miracle	*December 25, 1978*	**REG**
Reno Visitors Center	*September 9, 1984*	**RGJ**
Going, Going—Gone	*November 23, 1986*	**RGJ**
The Golden Rule	*March 9, 1980*	**REG**
The Little Big Fireman	*February 23, 1986*	**RGJ**
A Story of Romance	*April 20, 1987*	**RGJ**
Tangled Web of Names	*November 26, 1978*	**REG**
Bertha's Diet Story	*February 12, 1984*	**RGJ**

The Lighter Side

Good News	*October 14, 1979*	**REG**
Tall Tales Parents Tell	*December 31, 1978*	**REG**
My Fingers Did Some Walking	*June 24, 1979*	**REG**
Kay and the Snake	*September 23, 1981*	**REG**
K.B. Rao's Stories	*May 31, 1984*	**RGJ**
The Incredible Shrinking Bob	*February 25, 1979*	**REG**
Pooper-Scooper	*February 21, 1979*	**REG**
Otto's Diet	*September 24, 1980*	**REG**
A Rose Is a Rose	*November 8, 1978*	**REG**
Jordan and the Corks	*December 22, 1986*	**RGJ**
Infamous October	*November 6, 1978*	**REG**

Pages from the Past

A Day of Infamy	*December 7, 1981*	**REG**
The Men Who Built Hoover Dam	*June 12, 1983*	**RGJ**
The Campus Presidents Return	*May 21, 1984*	**RGJ**
Sagebrush Editors' Reunion	*September 8, 1986*	**RGJ**
A Man and His Music	*February 6, 1984*	**RGJ**
"Pappy"	*May 27, 1979*	**REG**

Nevada Profiles

He Wants to Quit Winners	*June 17, 1979*	**REG**
Choosing a Campus Leader	*March 21, 1979*	**REG**
Nevadan Fred Anderson	*February 2, 1986*	**RGJ**
Lyle Ball—Nevada Artist	*September 11, 1986*	**RGJ**
The Abortion Fighter	*March 30, 1980*	**REG**
Portrait of a Photographer	*August 14, 1983*	**RGJ**
Ben Dasher	*October 17, 1982*	**RGJ**
Agent Burau of the FBI	*August 5, 1979*	**REG**
A Visit with Governor Russell	*December 27, 1978*	**REG**

In Memoriam

Against Great Odds	*January 14, 1979*	**REG**
The Story of Mia	*August 3, 1983*	**RGJ**
A Prayer for Clare	*November 2, 1986*	**RGJ**
Editor Paul Leonard	*March 30, 1987*	**RGJ**
Mary Gojack	*November 17, 1985*	**RGJ**
Reporter's Reporter	*June 7, 1984*	**RGJ**
Woman of Distinction	*April 4, 1979*	**REG**
It Was Meant to Be	*December 8, 1985*	**RGJ**

Nevada Sports

Football Memories	*September 16, 1979*	**REG**
The Lunatic Factory	*October 21, 1979*	**REG**
Football Shoes	*September 24, 1979*	**REG**

Basketball Memories	*March 5, 1979*	**REG**
Jake Lawlor	*July 14, 1980*	**REG**
Jimmie Olivas Returns	*February 4, 1980*	**REG**
An Idol, Jack Dempsey, Dies	*June 6, 1983*	**RGJ**

Glimpses of the Famous

Meeting Patrick McCarran	*February 27, 1984*	**RGJ**
President Carter	*December 17, 1978*	**REG**
Phyllis Diller's Advice	*March 22, 1984*	**RGJ**
Dinner with Mr. Vice-President	*September 28, 1986*	**RGJ**

Faith, Hope and Charity

Town Without Strangers	*March 3, 1980*	**REG**
An Easter Story	*April 6, 1980*	**REG**
A Freakish Turning Point	*June 21, 1981*	**REG**
Anita's Caring Heart	*September 10, 1984*	**RGJ**
Requests for Christmas	*December 12, 1985*	**RGJ**
Helping Mary Jane	*April 26, 1987*	**RGJ**
Only Love to Give	*November 16, 1980*	**REG**
A Rescued Life	*November 27, 1986*	**RGJ**

Strictly Personal

The Story of Mel	*September 19, 1979*	**REG**
Annie	*May 21, 1980*	**REG**
The Curiosity of Grandchildren	*January 16, 1986*	**RGJ**
Grandpa Moses	*December 1, 1980*	**REG**
Say it Isn't So!	*January 16, 1981*	**REG**
The Lethal Habit	*November 21, 1985*	**RGJ**
A Story that Will Do Your Heart Good	*October 10, 1982*	**RGJ**
Not His Best Day	*January 27, 1986*	**RGJ**
Loving Each Newspaper Day	*April 19, 1987*	**RGJ**

INDEX

267